Conquest of the Atlantic
pioneer flights 1919–1939

by
Phil Munson

Stenlake Publishing
2002

Contents

© Phil Munson 2002
First published in the United Kingdom, 2002,
by Stenlake Publishing
Telephone / Fax: 01290 551122

ISBN 1 84033 180 1

Acknowledgements

This book is based on a talk given by myself and my good friend Mrs Audrey Wright to the Croydon Airport Society and Selsdon Camera Club. Without their interest, help and encouragement it would never have been written. In addition I would like to thank my wife Marion, especially for her patience whilst the decorating jobs piled up and also Doug Bastin, Peter Little and Oliver van Helden. The photograph of in-flight refuelling on page 67 was kindly provided by C. Crudas from the archive of Cobham PLC.

Author's note

Many of the details concerning pioneer transatlantic aviation vary between published sources – dates, distances and aircraft specifications are frequently inconsistent – particularly with regard to less well-known flights. Wherever possible, details have been corroborated by referring to several sources.

Introduction

The first flight of the *Hindenberg*, March 1936.

The story of the first attempts to fly across the Atlantic goes back to 1913 when Lord Northcliffe offered a £10,000 prize in his *Daily Mail* newspaper to anyone who could complete a non-stop flight between North America and Britain or Ireland (or vice versa). At the time this was both a huge amount of money and an incredibly daunting prospect. Aviation was still in its infancy, and most aircraft were made of wood, canvas and wire. Navigational aids were rudimentary, and radios (largely the preserve of military aircraft) were heavy, expensive and unreliable. Even magnetic compasses could not be relied upon, as they were often affected by petrol tanks and other metal parts. The early pilots were adventurers who took huge risks, especially as vital data such as maximum take-off weight and fuel consumption was generally not known.

The outbreak of the First World War in 1914 simultaneously scuppered any immediate prospect of the Northcliffe prize being claimed and provided an impetus for the development of aircraft for war use. By the time the war ended, aircraft were more advanced and the number of individuals and teams prepared to have a go at an Atlantic flight had increased.

When John Alcock and Arthur Whitten Brown landed in Ireland on 15 June 1919, claiming the Northcliffe prize, they achieved a huge feat. However, there were many more Atlantic milestones yet to be gained and many men (and a number of women) carried on where they had left off. Crashes and crash-landings were frequent, and aviators were often killed. Others were more fortunate, however, and there were extraordinary rescues too.

The first section of this book charts pioneer Atlantic attempts made in conventional aircraft up until 1939, by which time the first modern commercial airliner had made an Atlantic flight. The second section deals with airships, which for a while seemed to provide the perfect solution to long distance travel. The section on catapult mail looks at another aspect of transatlantic flight – delivering valuable payloads to their destinations as quickly as possible. Finally, a short section is devoted to some of the important flights that were made across the South Atlantic.

The men and women featured in this book range from household names such as Charles Lindbergh and Amy Johnson, to obscure adventurers like Bert Hinkler and Douglas Corrigan. These less well-known names are as important to the story as their famous counterparts. The cumulative expertise and experience gathered by numerous largely forgotten amateurs was of vital importance to those who made successful flights and became famous.

With very few exceptions, the illustrations in this book are reproduced from postcards collected by the author over more than 25 years. As a source of material, these have yielded many unusual and interesting artefacts, including cards carried on pioneer flights and signed by early aviators. However, as a result of limiting myself almost exclusively to postcard material, there are gaps in the story. Certain individuals, such as Beryl Markham, the first lady to make a solo flight across the Atlantic from east to west (the hard way!) should be featured, but I have not been able to track them down. Nonetheless, I hope I have managed to capture the spirit of the early Atlantic aviators and convey some of their pioneering spirit in the following pages.

Further reading

The books listed below were used by the author during his research. None of them are available from Stenlake Publishing. Those interested in finding out more are advised to contact their local bookshop or reference library.

1927, Summer of the Eagles, Jack Huttig, Nelson Hall, 1980

Airliners Between the Wars, Kenneth Munson, Blandford Press, 1972

Airship Saga, Lord Ventry & E. M. Kolesnik, Blandford Press, 1982

Airship, The Story of the R34, Patrick Abbott, Brewin Books, 1973

American Icarus – The Majestic Rise and Tragic Fall of PanAm, Jack E. Robinson, Noble House, 1994

Atlantic Air Conquest, F. H. & E. Ellis, William Kimber, 1963

Atlantic Wings, Kenneth McDonough, Modern Aeronautical Press, 1966

Chronicle of Aviation, J. L. International Publishing, n.d.

Croydon Airport, The Great Days, Bob Learmonth et al., Sutton Libraries, 1980

Flying Boats and Seaplanes, Kenneth Munson, Blandford Press, 1971

Lindbergh, Leonard Mosley, Doubleday & Co., 1976

Lindbergh Alone, Brendan Gill, Harcourt Brace Jovanovich, 1977

Lufthansa, An Airline and its Aircraft, R. E. G. Davies, Orion Books, 1991

Mollison, The Flying Scotsman, David Luff, Lidun Publishing, 1993

Pan American's Ocean Clippers, Barry Taylor, Flying Classics Series, 1990

Pan Am, An Airline and its Aircraft, R. E. G. Davis, Hamlyn, 1987

R101, A Pictorial History, Nick Le Neve Walmsley, Sutton Publishing Ltd., 2000

Revolution in the Sky, Richard Sanders Allen, Orion Books/New York, 1988

Slide Rule, Neville Shute, Pan Books, 1954

The Conquest of the Atlantic by Air, Charles Dixon, Sampson Low, Marston, 1930

The First Croydon Airport, Bob Learmonth et al., Sutton Libraries, 1977

The Flight of Alcock and Brown, Graham Wallace, Putnam, 1955

The Great Atlantic Air Race, Percy Rowe, McClelland and Sterart, 1977

The Hero, Kenneth S. Davis, Longmans, 1960

The Last Flight of Bert Hinkler, Edward P. Wixted, Vantage Press, 1992

The North Atlantic Catapult, Roger Stanley Smith, Pier Point Publishing, 1990

The Pan Am Clipper, Roy Allen, David and Charles, 2000

The Zeppelin – The History of the German Airships 1900–1937, Christopher Chant, David and Charles, 2000

They Flew the Atlantic, Robert de la Croix, Frederick Muller, n.d.

Who's Who in Aviation History, William H. Longyard, Airlife, 1994

Wings Over the Atlantic, Robert J. Hoare, Phoenix House Ltd., 1956

World Aircraft 1918–1935, Angelucci/Matricardi, Sampson Low Guides, 1977

North Atlantic flights

In 1913 Lord Northcliffe, the proprietor of the *Daily Mail* newspaper, offered a prize of £10,000 to the first person to make a direct flight across the North Atlantic between any point in the British Isles and any point in Newfoundland, Canada or the United States. The flight was to be completed within 72 hours and could be made in either direction. Although the prize money was a vast amount in those days, the difficulties that would be faced during such a flight were formidable, and thought by some to be insurmountable. One newspaper appealed to Lord Northcliffe to cancel the prize for the sake of humanity before lives were lost. Another, out of ridicule, announced it would increase the prize money to £1 million. Luckily for them, this was not a firm offer. One of the first to accept the challenge was Glenn Curtiss.

At the time, Curtiss was considered to be the most important American aviator after the Wright brothers. He had become famous as a motorcyclist, and in 1907 set a new world land speed record of 136.3 miles per hour on a motorcycle of his own design. The following year he made the first official public flight in the USA in his aircraft *June Bug*, and in 1909 won the world famous Gordon Bennett Cup for aviation at Reims. It is interesting to compare the aircraft illustrated here, in which he won $2,000 for a long-distance flight in 1910, with the flying boat *America* which he hoped to fly the Atlantic in only four years later.

Glenn Curtiss.

Curtiss and one of his biplanes.

The Curtiss *America*.

The Curtiss *America*, a very advanced aircraft for its time, was sponsored by Rodman Wannamaker, a millionaire US store owner. First tests of the aircraft were promising, and it was reported that an attempt to fly from Newfoundland to Ireland would be made on 15 or 16 July 1914. However, the original two-engined design did not provide sufficient power for take-off, and when an additional engine was fitted it was calculated that the fuel consumption would be too high for a direct flight. Before further modifications could be carried out, the project was abandoned due to the outbreak of war in Europe.

Glenn Curtiss had intended to be the pilot on the Atlantic flight, but his wife forbade him. An Irishman, Cyril John Porte, was selected in his place, and deservedly so as he had been of great assistance to Curtiss in the design and construction of the *America*. Born in 1884, Porte had previously served on submarines in the British Navy. He was invalidated out with tuberculosis, and after recovering joined the Royal Naval Air Service, learning to fly in 1910.

Cyril John Porte seated in an unidentified aircraft.

Porte (with hand on hip) photographed alongside the *America* during its naming ceremony.

In 1916 the Curtiss *America* was sold to Great Britain for use in the war effort, and Porte accompanied the aircraft across the Atlantic on the liner *Mauretania*. British flying boats used in the war were largely based on the *America*, and Porte was a key figure in designing and constructing a whole range of these, designated F1 to F5. The F4, a massive five-engined triplane called the *Felixstowe Fury*, was once the largest aircraft in the world. A seven hour flight during which 24 passengers were carried made it a possible contender for an Atlantic crossing, but it crashed on a later test flight in 1919.

Porte barely survived the war, a victim of his recurrent tuberculosis, but in spite of this made a great contribution to the war effort, not only through his design work but both as a test and bomber pilot. Lieutenant Colonel (Wing Commander) Porte died in 1919 aged 35. He lived just long enough to welcome the crew of NC-4, the first aircraft to fly the Atlantic, on their arrival at Plymouth in May that year.

The *Felixstowe Fury*.

In 1918, after the end of the war, Lord Northcliffe's *Daily Mail* again offered its prize of £10,000 for the first Atlantic flight. Initially there were eleven entries, although only five finally took up the challenge. Four elected to start from Newfoundland to take advantage of favourable winds, and their aircraft were transported from the UK on ships including the Furness liners *Glendevon* and *Digby*. The fifth contender, called the *Shamrock*, intended to fly from Ireland but crashed in the sea off Holyhead before it got there. The crew were saved.

In Newfoundland there was frantic activity to prepare makeshift airfields. The local workforce found that vast sums of money could be made from this work and also from housing the aviators and mechanics. On their arrival in Newfoundland the aircraft were taken – often with the aid of horses – to these airfields. They were then assembled in very primitive conditions, frequently in tents or the open air.

Furness Liner "Glendevon" which conveyed to Newfoundland the Vickers' Aeroplane in which Sir John Alcock made the first successful Trans-Atlantic Flight.

Loading a Handley-Page Aeroplane on Furness Liner "Digby"

Amidst all this activity, it was announced that a team from the United States Navy intended to attempt to fly the Atlantic. They would not compete for Lord Northcliffe's prize as they planned to break their flight at the Azores. Their project seems to have followed the first theorem of US organisation: Throw enough money at the problem and maybe you can't fail! Four Navy Curtiss flying boats were to be used, plus an airship, C-5. However, the enthusiastic Americans forgot the second theorem: Any increase in the amount of organisation, men and machinery in a project drastically increases the chance of failure. The four flying boats were numbered NC-1 to NC-4 and on 27 November 1918 the prototype, NC-1, created a world record by carrying 51 people (including a stowaway) on a test flight. (After this flight it was found that the control column had been incorrectly assembled and it was a miracle that the aircraft had not crashed.) In March 1919 NC-1 was badly damaged in a storm but was repaired using parts from the incomplete NC-2. NC-4 also had problems. On 30 April 1919, her first occasion afloat, she took 80 gallons of water on board through leaks and sustained damage to the hull and wing support struts. Worse still, on 5 May 1919 NC-1 and NC-4 were badly damaged in a hangar fire. Both aircraft were repaired with yet more parts from NC-2.

The Navy Curtiss carried a crew of six, with the commander (navigator) located in an open cockpit in the bow getting very cold and wet. The two pilots, who were required to control the aircraft by sheer brute strength most of the time, were in another open cockpit behind him with two engineers and a radio operator in the rear cockpit. None of the cockpits had any heating, and no parachutes were provided. The engineers were fitted with lifelines so they could climb about on the wings and work on the engines during flight.

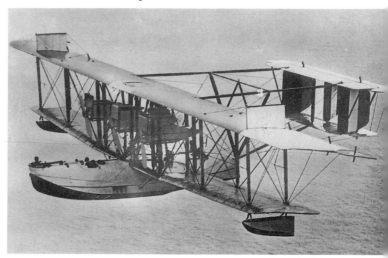

NC-9, a similar aircraft to the Navy Curtiss flying boats used by the American team.

NC-4 AND PART OF CREW

On 8 May 1919 NC-1, NC-3 and NC-4 left Rockaway, New Jersey on the first stage of their journey – to Halifax, Nova Scotia. The next stage was to Trepassey Bay, Newfoundland. From there, the American Navy tried to ensure the aircraft would not get lost on their journey by positioning over 50 warships at 50 mile intervals along the entire route to England via the Azores and Lisbon. These made smoke by day and were orientated in the direction of flight. At night they used searchlights, again to indicate the line of flight. They also fired star shells and rockets, nearly shooting down one aircraft in the process.

NC-1 and NC-3 made it to Halifax, and on to Trepassey Bay. NC-4, soon to become known as the 'lame duck', was not so lucky. Two engines failed and the aircraft was forced to taxi 80 miles to Chatham, Massachusetts for

repairs. Another engine failed before reaching Trepassey Bay. On the journey the crew were surprised to see an airship blowing out to sea, obviously out of control. This was C-5, which the US Navy had flown in secret to St John's, Newfoundland, and which was also to attempt to fly the Atlantic. Unfortunately it had broken loose in a storm and had blown away, to be lost forever. Upon arrival at Trepassey Bay, the crew of NC-4 saw the other two aircraft vainly trying to take off fully loaded from the open sea, apparently having spent the whole afternoon doing this. NC-4 had already experienced the same problem and the crew had worked out how to overcome it. They had discovered by trial and error that the gauges on the fuel tanks were not accurate. Due to them giving a falsely low reading, more fuel was taken on board than the aircraft could actually lift.

The US marker ships positioned between Newfoundland and the Azores.

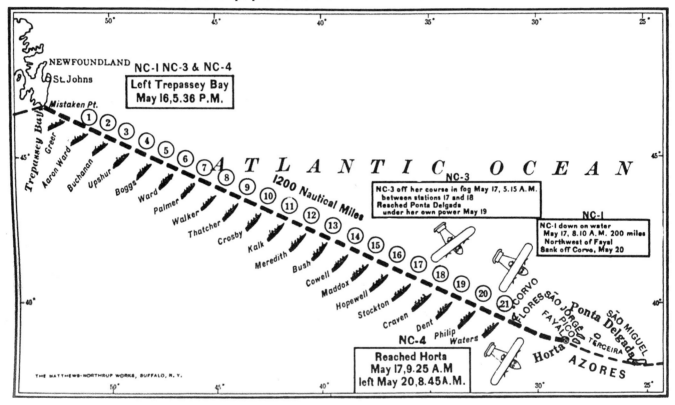

NC-4, the 'lame duck'.

Eventually, the three aircraft managed to take off from Trepassey Bay for the Azores on 16 May after leaving behind some fuel and a crew member. Commander Towers of NC-3 had also offloaded some equipment, including the emergency radio transmitter. Soon after take-off, in bad visibility, the three aircraft converged on a marker ship at the same time, only just avoiding collision (navigation lights had yet to be invented). Having averted this disaster, they soon got separated and lost in fog and low cloud. Worse still, the 21 warships marking this stage of the route proved hard to find. If a ship was not seen after about half an hour, a sense of panic set in and there was a temptation to alter course and go looking for it. Totally lost, the commander of NC-1, afraid of crashing into mountains on the Azores, tried to land his aircraft on the open sea. He thought he would be able to find his position better at sea level, but the aircraft was badly damaged on impact and was unable to take off again. After five hours the crew were picked up by the Greek cargo ship *Ionia* and taken to the Azores. The American warship *Fairfax* later managed to get a towline to the stricken NC-1, but she turned turtle and sank.

The commander of NC-3 also tried to land on the sea. On impact his aircraft's hull split open and a wing and float were badly damaged. Two crewmen had to lie lashed to the end of the damaged wing to stop the aircraft from capsizing. A makeshift sail was rigged up, and unable to send out a distress signal as they had left their radio transmitter behind, the crew drifted 200 miles in 53 hours before the Azores came into sight. On approaching land, they started up their engines and proudly made their way into harbour.

Fairfax attempting to save the stricken NC-1.

NC-3 limping into Ponta Delgada, Azores.

Hidro-avião N. C. 3 entrando no porto depois da travessia do Atlantico. Parte leste de Ponta Delgada (Açores)

Despite her disparaging nickname, NC-4 reached the Azores without any problems. When all three crews met up, a blazing row erupted. As the highest ranking officer, Commander Towers of NC-3 expected to take over NC-4. However, the American public were incensed at this, and eventually the saga reached the White House. From on high it was decided that Lieutenant Commander Read (US Naval Aviator No. 24) of NC-4 should retain command for the flight to England. This was the second disappointment as far as Commander Towers (US Naval Aviator No. 3) was concerned. He had been selected for the 1914 trans-atlantic attempt as co-pilot to Curtiss, who in 1911 had

taught him to fly. Instead he was sent to serve in the border war between the United States and Mexico.

NC-4 had reached Ponta Delgada, Azores on 17 May but was delayed there by bad weather until 27 May when she left for Lisbon, which she reached the same day. Read had initially been worried that one of two pairs of contenders for Lord Northcliffe's prize would beat him to England, but when both their attempts failed the sense of urgency lessened. Fourteen US Navy ships were lined up as markers along the 800 mile route to Lisbon, from where NC-4 continued her journey on 30 May, landing at Figueira, Portugal and Ferrol, Spain en route to Plymouth.

NC-4 in Lisbon harbour.

NC-4 at Plymouth.

At 9.26 a.m. on 31 May 1919, NC-4 reached Plymouth to a great welcome. The crew had flown over 4,000 miles in 54 hours, although this was spread over 23 days. It was a long time before the row between Towers and Read subsided. It lasted throughout their distinguished careers in World War II, which led to both being promoted to the rank of admiral (Towers was the first naval aviator to reach this rank). With time, however, it is said that it became more like the famous Bing Crosby and Bob Hope relationship. In 1979 I travelled from Miami to New York by bus, partly with the aim of seeing historic aircraft. On reaching the Smithsonian Museum in Washington, hoping to see NC-4, I was told it was undergoing restoration back in Florida!

The crew of NC-4 being greeted by the Mayor of Plymouth, 31 May 1919.

Now back to the challenge for Lord Northcliffe's prize. By May 1919 four aircraft and crews had assembled in Newfoundland and were waiting for better weather conditions before commencing their flights. Of these the first away were Harry Hawker and Kenneth Mackenzie-Grieve on 18 May 1919. Australian Harry Hawker had been employed during World War I on the design and test-flying of aircraft, including the Sopwith Triplane fighter. He had also broken records for duration and high altitude flights. His navigator, Lieutenant Commander Mackenzie-Grieve, had gained aero-navigation experience on a seaplane carrier during the war.

Harry Hawker.

Their specially designed Sopwith, called *Atlantic*, used parts from existing aircraft and was built in about six weeks. It was powered by a 375 h.p. Rolls Royce Eagle engine, and a small lifeboat was built into the fuselage. To save weight and drag, the undercarriage would be jettisoned after take-off, and the aircraft was designed to be belly-landed at the end of its flight.

The first indications of trouble during the flight came from the water temperature gauge, which showed an abnormally high reading. It was discovered that this could be rectified by diving from about 12,000 to 9,000 feet so that the cold airflow cooled the water. This trick was used several times, but each time the temperature ultimately climbed higher. Also, the extra fuel consumption required to climb back up to 12,000 feet jeopardised their chances of reaching land. Later, the overheating engine began to misfire and then finally cut out, forcing them to land on the sea.

The Sopwith *Atlantic*.

SAVED!

Mr. H. HAWKER, the brave airman who, with COMMANDER GRIEVE, R.N., who started on the Atlantic Flight from Newfoundland on Sunday May 18th. 1919.   The attempt was unsuccessful.

News that Hawker and Mackenzie-Grieve were missing was greeted with great dismay in Britain. In spite of an extensive search by the Royal Navy and RAF, by Sunday 25 May, a week after they had taken off, all hope had been lost and the nation went into mourning. Prayers were said throughout the land and the King sent a telegram of condolence to Mrs Hawker. Then, great news! They were discovered safe! A Danish tramp steamer, *Mary*, which was not equipped with radio, flag-signalled to a coastguard station in Scotland that the gallant airmen were alive and well. They had landed near the *Mary* and launched their lifeboat, and after a very difficult rescue ended up safely on board ship. After being picked up by the Royal Navy and taken to Thurso, they travelled to London by train. Their journey became a triumphant procession, with great crowds greeting them at stations along the route. At Grantham, in the privacy of a small room at the railway station, Hawker had a joyous reunion with his wife. She had never given up hope that he would be saved.

PHOTO BY
DAILY MIRROR.

MR. H. G. HAWKER'S JOYOUS ARRIVAL IN LONDON.
AFTER HIS ATLANTIC FLIGHT.

168.G.
BEAGLES' POSTCARDS.

**'Mr H. G. Hawker's homecoming.
A "joy ride" through the crowd.'**

When the train carrying Hawker and Mackenzie-Grieve pulled into King's Cross station, the surrounding streets were thronged with people waiting to greet them. Before the airmen had time to meet the official welcoming party, Hawker was grabbed and carried shoulder high out of the station by several hundred of his fellow Australians – servicemen waiting to return home after the war. He and his wife were put in a Sunbeam car and dragged through the streets in it at the head of a frenzied procession.

Hawker began to fear for his safety, and was eventually rescued by a policeman on horseback. The following morning the two men were received at Buckingham Palace by King George V and Prince Albert (later King George VI). They were invested with the Air Force Cross. This was a particular honour for Hawker, as it was the first time the cross had been awarded to a civilian. At a reception at the Savoy Hotel, they were presented with a £5,000 consolation prize awarded by Lord Northcliffe. In spite of a previous arrangement that Hawker should get 70 per cent of any prize money, he insisted that his navigator received an equal share of this award.

The *Atlantic* on Selfridge's roof.

Their aircraft was eventually picked up by an American ship, *Lake Charlotteville*, and taken to Falmouth and from there to London. After being displayed on Selfridge's roof, the *Atlantic* was transported to Southport and exhibited in a large marquee where over 12,000 people paid to see it. Unfortunately, souvenir hunters helped themselves to anything removable whilst the policeman on duty was 'spending a penny'. Soon afterwards the marquee blew down in a gale and the aircraft was finished off for good.

Hawker resumed his aviation career and also raced cars, speedboats and motorcycles. He subsequently formed the Hawker Engineering Company, the forerunner of the famous Hawker Aeroplane Company, with Sopwith. In 1920 he was diagnosed with tuberculosis of the spine, but in spite of great pain and suffering endeavoured to continue his test-flying and racing activities. He was killed aged 32 in an accident in July 1921 while test-flying the British Nieuport Company's Goshawk. Kenneth Mackenzie-Grieve evaded the limelight and slipped into obscurity. In 1942 he died in British Columbia at the age of 62.

'Mr & Mrs H. G. Hawker & Com. Grieve. All smiles after the Atlantic flight.'

Only two hours after Hawker and Mackenzie-Grieve's departure on 18 May 1919, their main rivals took off in pursuit. Freddie Raynham and 'Fax' Morgan's Martinsyde aircraft *Raymor* was faster than Hawker's *Atlantic* and they hoped to overtake him en route. To overcome the stress of not knowing whether the other team were going on a test flight or an actual attempt, there had been a gentlemen's agreement between the teams to give two hours notice of an actual flight. Morgan hoped that his faster aircraft would get to the UK first, but for the second time since their arrival *Raymor* crashed on take-off and the injuries sustained meant an end to his and Raynham's attempt.

Meanwhile, John Alcock and Arthur Whitten Brown were still waiting for their aircraft to arrive. Both Alcock and Brown had joined the Royal Flying Corps on the outbreak of war in 1914. By coincidence both were shot down and held prisoner for the duration of the war. However, they did not meet until Brown applied for work at the Vickers Aeroplane Company where Alcock was a test pilot. At the time, Alcock was urgently seeking a navigator for a proposed Atlantic flight. Brown, who had studied navigation whilst a prisoner of war, made an ideal partner.

On arrival in Newfoundland on board the SS *Glendevon* on 13 May, their Vickers Vimy had to be reassembled. This took thirteen days, with most of the work carried out in the open air under extreme conditions of wind, rain, ice and snow. A test flight took place on 9 June and the transatlantic attempt was made on 14 June. Great difficulty was had in finding a field long enough for the take-off run, and in fact the one that was chosen almost proved to be too short. After the vastly overloaded aircraft struggled into the air, onlookers got a great fright as it disappeared from view into a valley just beyond the take-off point. Alcock and Brown soon experienced further problems. Their radio set was powered by a small generator driven by a propellor, which fell off shortly after take-off. Both men were wearing electrically-heated suits to keep them warm in their open cockpit, and these stopped working. Part of an exhaust broke off, and fog, snow and rain made navigation almost impossible.

Alcock and Brown.

Alcock and Brown's Vickers Vimy taking off on its record-breaking Atlantic flight.

The Vickers Vimy after landing in marshy ground on the Irish coast.

The men's worst moment came when their aircraft stalled and fell in a spiral for several thousand feet. Alcock lost his sense of direction, but the sea became visible enabling him to regain control at the last moment. Then, on the morning of 15 June 1919, about sixteen hours after take-off, they reached the Irish coast near Clifden and chose a likely landing space which they thought was a field. Their aircraft finished up with its nose buried in marshy ground, but the crew were not injured and they had much to celebrate. They were the first people to have flown non-stop across the Atlantic.

After a civic reception at Galway that afternoon, and another in Dublin the following day, Alcock and Brown boarded a boat for Holyhead and travelled by train to London. Brown's fiancee, Kathleen Kennedy, joined the train at Rugby. At a lunch given in their honour at the Royal Aero Club, Winston Churchill presented them with their £10,000 prize and announced that the King had granted them immediate knighthoods. Other receptions followed, including one at Weybridge where their Vickers Vimy had been built, and where they were made especially welcome.

The welcome reception at Weybridge.

THE VICKERS-VIMY MACHINE.

Lieutenant Arthur Brown and Captain John Alcock.

On 15 December 1919, Alcock and Brown saw the Vimy presented to the nation at the Science Museum in London, where it is on display to this day. Three days later Sir John Alcock was dead, having been killed in a flying accident whilst delivering a Vickers Viking aircraft to Paris. Brown never flew again, possibly because of the traumas he had experienced during the flight or the tragic death of his comrade. He faded from the limelight, and was employed in Swansea by the Metro Vickers Company as a sales manager. His world crumbled when his only son was killed on active service in 1944 and he committed suicide in 1948.

AMERICAN EXPEDITION LEAVE SANTA MONICA FOR WORLD FLIGHT

During the First World War responsibility for American military aviation was shared between the Air Service (a small part of the army), and the navy. There was no separate air force as such. After the war the defence budget was drastically reduced, and Major General Patrick, commander of the Air Service, realised that to maximise his share of the budget he would have to gain the support of the American public. He decided that the best way of doing this was by means of newsworthy flights. These included such things as altitude and long distance record flights, and flights between cities. One such flight was made between New York and San Diego in just under 27 hours. However, the ultimate challenge was a round the world flight, and this was attempted in 1924 using four American Douglas World Cruisers (DWCs). The flight officially commenced from Seattle on 6 April 1924.

20

This postcard of *New Orleans* is the only known souvenir of the American round the world flight from Karachi.

Specially designed and built for the flight, the World Cruiser carried a crew of two and had a cruising speed of 103 m.p.h. at 10,000 feet. The four aircraft were given names of American cities that approximately represented the four compass points: No.1, *Seattle* (west); No. 2, *Chicago* (north); No. 3, *Boston* (east); No. 4, *New Orleans* (south). The vast amount of preparatory work and planning required for the flight took over a year. Arrangements for landing were made at over 70 places in 23 foreign nations, and complete spares kits, each containing 480 items and intended to include everything likely to be needed, were prepared. These kits, plus no less than 35 engines, were shipped to strategic points along the route. Arrangements were made for wheels to be replaced by floats for flights over water. Plans were also made so that nearly all flight stages could be completed during daylight.

Flying from east to west via Canada, Alaska, Japan and China, three of the aircraft reached Karachi on 4 July 1924 where they were overhauled and fitted with new engines by the RAF. One aircraft, *Seattle*, had been lost when it crashed into a mountain in Alaska, although the crew were rescued. By the time they reached Paris, the remaining crews were getting very tired; one contemporary account says they fell asleep during a performance at the Follies Bergere. Eventually the three aircraft reached Croydon on 16 July having flown over 17,500 miles. However, they soon left for the Blackburn aircraft factory at Brough, Yorkshire, where they were overhauled and fitted with floats for the last stages of their journey back to the US via Iceland, Greenland and Canada.

New Orleans **photographed at Hinaidi, Iraq.**

The flight between Scotland and Iceland nearly ended in disaster when the aircraft ran into a fog bank and lost sight of each other. *New Orleans* was unbalanced by the prop-wash from one of the other aircraft and fell into a spinning dive, recovering just before hitting the sea. Later, *Boston's* engine failed and it was forced to land on the sea. Its crew were rescued by a warship but the aircraft was lost. The two remaining DWCs, *New Orleans* and *Chicago*, reached Nova Scotia on 3 September. Here they were joined by Leigh Wade and Henry Ogden, the crew of *Boston*. As they had come so close to completing their flight round the world, the prototype World Cruiser was hastily renamed *Boston II* so that they could finish the flight. *New Orleans* and *Chicago* finally reached Seattle on 28 September after 175 days away from home. They had flown over 27,000 miles in fifteen days actual flying time.

Rare photographs of *Chicago* taken at Hinaidi, Iraq, in 1924.

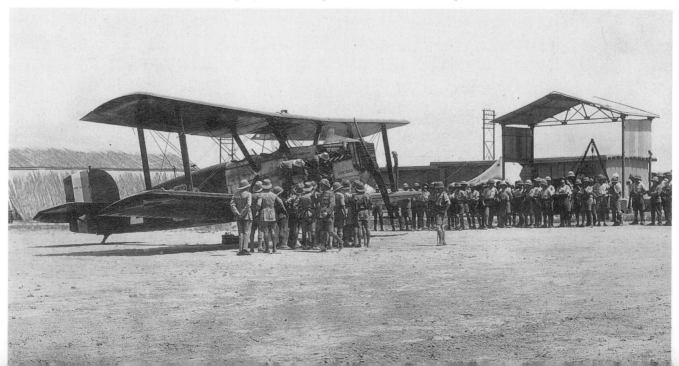

Interest in Atlantic flights was sustained by a $25,000 prize put up by millionaire hotelier Raymond Orteig for the first direct flight linking New York and Paris. Although originally offered in 1919, the challenge was not taken up until 1926 due to lack of suitable aircraft. At the time the prize money was equivalent to an average American's wages for 50 years. The first contender, in September 1926, was French ace pilot Rene Fonck in a Sikorsky S35 three-engined biplane. Weight had been a problem with his aircraft from the outset, and with the necessary fuel-load of 2,380 gallons on board it finished up 10,000 lbs heavier than its designed weight. Igor Sikorsky, the designer, proposed a series of test flights to establish a safe maximum take-off weight but Fonck refused his request, frightened that he may be beaten to Paris. Savings could have been made by dispensing with the expensive and bulky finishings in the cabin. These included a red leather couch that converted to a bed,

carpeting, curtains, and an insulated food cupboard containing pre-cooked victuals for a celebration banquet at Paris. During their take-off from Roosevelt airfield on 20 September 1926, an auxiliary trolley, designed to be released when the aircraft was airborne, collapsed, damaging the elevators. The aircraft crashed in rough ground at the end of the runway. Fonck and his co-pilot jumped clear but the mechanic and radio operator both burned to death.

On 26 April 1927 a three-engined Keystone Pathfinder – another vastly overloaded aircraft – failed to take off. The crew, US Navy Lieutenant Commander Noel Davis and his co-pilot Stanton Wooster, drowned in four feet of water when their aircraft hit trees and crashed in a swamp. The plane had exceeded design calculations and when delivered was already more than half a ton overweight. The pair were also trying to win the Orteig prize.

A postcard entitled 'Another trans-atlantic plane crash. Lt. Cdr. Noel Davis & Lt. Wooster killed.'

Nungesser and Coli and *L'Oiseau Blanc*.

In the same year that Davis and Wooster perished on their transatlantic attempt, two French airmen, Charles Nungesser and Francois Coli, decided on a Paris to New York flight, even though battling against headwinds would make their task still more difficult. Their aircraft, a Levasseur PL.8 single-engine biplane called *L'Oiseau Blanc* (White Bird) was capable of maintaining 125 m.p.h. for 40 hours, thought to be sufficient to complete the flight with ease. To save weight the undercarriage would be jettisoned after take-off. The fuselage was designed to float on water for a considerable time in the event of a crash landing.

Charles Nungesser had had a very successful career as a fighter pilot during the First World War with 45 'kills' to his credit. On the other hand many injuries suffered in aircraft and motoring accidents meant that it was said that, on occasion, the only way to get him to and from his plane was to carry him in a chair. After the war he left France for America. He became a stunt pilot in flying circuses and an actor in adventure films. His navigator, Francois Coli, also had a distinguished war record.

On 8 May 1927 the men loaded their aircraft with supplies, including a two-week stock of bananas, caviar, fish-hooks and a small can of bait. No radio was carried. As was quite common on flights such as theirs, they had no idea of the aircraft's maximum take-off weight. Taking off with a full load of fuel was considered too dangerous to try more than once. As a safety factor, however, in view of a favourable weather forecast, they reduced their fuel load.

At first all seemed well. After take-off, the undercarriage was jettisoned and can now be seen on display in the Musée de l'Air at Le Bourget near Paris. The aircraft was escorted as far as the French coast and then faded from view. Hours later reports reached New York that *L'Oiseau Blanc* had been seen over Newfoundland and later Boston. News bulletins even described the two men's arrival in New York. Then there was silence and it was reluctantly announced that the aircraft was missing. Offloading extra fuel before take-off was probably their undoing. After *L'Oiseau Blanc* passed from sight an updated weather report showed that it would run out of fuel more than 300 miles from America. There was no way of warning Nungesser and Coli and the gallant airmen were never seen again. Over the years there have been reports of wreckage being found in Maine, as well as off the French coast and in Newfoundland.

Nungesser's First World War flying insignia were painted on the side of *L'Oiseau Blanc*.

This memorial was erected at Etretat, where Nungesser and Coli were last seen over French soil.

Towards the end of 1926, preparations for New York to Paris flights were reaching fever pitch. The favourite contender was Commander (later Admiral) Richard Byrd in a three-engined Fokker, a similar aircraft to the one in which he had made the first flight to the North Pole in May 1926. Second favourite was Charles Levine's aircraft, *Miss Columbia* (generally known as *Columbia*), designed by Giuseppe Bellanca and built by the Wright Corporation. The main feature of this aircraft was its curved fuselage and the aerofoil-like shape of the wing and undercarriage struts which gave it exceptional lifting powers. This, coupled with the fact that the Wright Whirlwind engine was the most reliable and economical engine in the world, made it an ideal aircraft for an Atlantic flight.

Charles Levine's aircraft, *Columbia*.

Bellanca *Miss Columbia* — 1927

Charles Levine was a millionaire war surplus dealer who had started building his business empire at the age of twelve by selling scrap metal. A major source of income was said to have come from buying war surplus material from the American government and selling it back to them later. He bought *Columbia* with the aim of operating the proposed New York to Chicago mail service. When he failed to get the contract, he founded the Columbia Aircraft Corporation, employing Bellanca to set up an aircraft production line.

To generate publicity for his new company Levine decided to compete for the Orteig prize. However, to demonstrate *Columbia*'s performance and reliability he first attempted to break the long-distance endurance record of the time. His chief pilot Clarence Chamberlin and co-pilot Bert Acosta easily achieved this, flying over 4,000 miles in 51 hours between 12 and 14 April 1927.

But however Levine had made his millions, it certainly wasn't as a result of his diplomacy. Arguments soon broke out between Levine, Chamberlin and Acosta, resulting in the latter resigning. Another pilot, Lloyd Bertaud, took Acosta's place but further arguments flared up, mainly over Levine's refusal to arrange life insurance for his pilots during the proposed Atlantic flight. Bertaud took out a court injunction against Levine preventing *Columbia* from flying to Paris without him. Although the aircraft was ready and waiting, Levine's problems gave other contenders extra time to prepare for their flights.

On 9 May 1926 Richard Byrd had made the first flight over the North Pole in the *Josephine Ford*. In June the same year it was announced that he intended to fly from New York to Paris to claim the Orteig prize. His attempt was sponsored by Rodman Wannamaker (who had sponsored the Curtiss *America* in 1914), who put up $10,000 to cover all expenses. By April 1927 his new Fokker aircraft had been completed, but on its first test flight (16 April) Anthony Fokker was persuaded to take Byrd and his two intended pilots for the Atlantic flight, Floyd Bennett and George Noville, with him in the three-seater cockpit. On landing the aircraft somersaulted and was badly damaged. Two crew members were injured. Some reports say the weight of the extra passenger moved the centre of gravity too far forward, although another theory is that the crash was caused by somebody obstructing the controls.

The *Josephine Ford*.

One contender who benefited from Levine's squabbling and Byrd's misfortune was Charles Lindbergh, a pilot on the St Louis to Chicago airmail route. Lindbergh realised that in the case of Rene Fonck's abortive transatlantic attempt, the aircraft had been too big and heavy. With three engines there was a greater likelihood of engine failure (and anyway, the plane couldn't fly for long on two engines). Lindbergh wondered whether it would be possible to make a solo flight across the ocean, thereby saving fuel, weight and space. It was a maxim that airmail flights had to be made in all weathers, and if a pilot could see to take off, the mail had to go. As a result airmail pilots were used to flying in adverse weather and could find their destinations by means of landmarks such as isolated farms or navigation beacons. Lindbergh could cope with emergencies, and on two occasions, having run out of fuel and unable to see well enough to land, had been forced to parachute to safety, leaving the mail and his aircraft to their fate. In both cases he recovered the mail and took it to its destination by train. He began to plan a solo Atlantic flight.

Charles Lindbergh.

40A:—Ryan's Flying School, San Diego, Calif.

Where Lindberg's famous flight began.

A statue of Lindbergh erected at the Ryan flying school and factory after his record-breaking flight.

Having approached a number of prominent businessmen in St Louis and obtained their financial backing, Lindbergh tried unsuccessfully to buy *Columbia* from the Wright Corporation. This request was refused, partly because he had never flown across an ocean before. Subsequently Lindbergh attempted to purchase the aircraft from Levine. The deal was agreed with a handshake and Lindbergh even picked up the cheque from the bank. Unfortunately Levine, typically unreliable, changed his mind at the last minute. Lindbergh suffered another setback when Anthony Fokker refused to build him an aircraft with less than three engines. In desperation he approached Ryan Airlines of San Diego instead.

Although partly based on an existing Ryan design, Lindbergh and the young, enthusiastic team at Ryan worked miracles in building the *Spirit of St Louis* in under three months. One problem was where to install the large additional fuel tank necessary for the Atlantic flight. Finally it was positioned in front of the pilot's seat as Lindbergh did not want to be crushed by it in the event of an accident. This, however, impeded his forward vision and a small periscope was fitted to overcome this difficulty. Building the aircraft in what had originally been a cannery caused problems. At the last minute it was found that the undercarriage, which had been specially widened, would not pass through the door of the factory. The wing assembly was too long to bring down the stairs from the attic and had to be manhandled through a window to the ground via the roof of a railway boxcar.

Lindbergh photographed with members of the Ryan team and the *Spirit of St Louis*.

Von Hall Designer.   Col. Graham.
Capt. Lindbergh.
Mr. Edwards.

M.J. Ford Photo
Long Beach, Calif

Capt. Chas. Lindbergh just before the Hop-off.

Lindbergh was determined to keep the weight of his aircraft to the absolute minimum. In addition to his flying suit, he took a water flask and was persuaded to carry a small emergency kit including a life raft (which doubled as a cushion) and an 'Armburst' cup with which drinking water could be distilled from sea water. One personal item is not shown in this picture. This was an aluminium can in which he urinated, and which did not survive the flight. In *Lindbergh*, by Leonard Mosley, the author records that he threw it overboard before he reached Paris. That was a wise precaution, because after the flight there was a frantic demand for souvenirs of all sorts. Fabric was ripped from the aircraft and small components including nuts and bolts disappeared. Lindbergh had to punch someone quite violently to stop his helmet and goggles being snatched from his face. One theft, which Lindbergh regretted for the rest of his life, was the log book in which he'd detailed the flight.

Lindbergh's kit for his transatlantic flight.

OUR "LINDY"
Bidding Farewell to Renowned French Flyer, Rene Fouck, Before the Start

Rene Fonck, whose attempted flight to Paris the previous year had ended in disaster, came to see Lindbergh and wish him well. It was said that Fonck's skill and bravery had helped him to survive in the thick of battle for over two years during the First World War, shooting down a record 75 enemy aircraft. This was at a time when the average fighter pilot was lucky to last more than three weeks.

Rene Fonck was famous as being the smallest of the French air aces of the First World War.

Lindbergh, Byrd and Chamberlin. Byrd's left arm is in plaster, following the crash during the test flight.

On the evening of 19 May 1927 there was great excitement in New York. It was announced that Byrd had almost completed his test flights and hoped to leave for Paris the next day (although in the event he delayed his departure). The situation regarding Levine and his pilots was still very confused. It emerged that in addition to the life insurance problem, there had also been arguments between all three men about the proposed route, the provision of a radio set and other matters. Levine had offered to sell *Columbia* to Bertaud for $25,000 (twice the cost of Lindbergh's aircraft, *Spirit of St Louis*), but before Bertaud could raise the money he withdrew his offer. A new contract that was acceptable to Bertaud was drawn up, but later Levine refused to ratify it. The three main adversaries, Byrd, Chamberlin and Lindbergh, agreed to pose for the press. Rumour and speculation broke out when a newsman overheard Lindbergh cancel a dinner date on the phone and wrongly assumed a take-off was imminent. By 9 p.m. a special newspaper edition announcing his impending departure had hit the streets. In response to this, Levine phoned the papers and announced that *Columbia* would leave at daybreak. However, at 1.30 a.m., in view of bad weather reports, Chamberlin told the press that *Columbia* wouldn't fly.

Meanwhile, Lindbergh was experiencing the familiar problem of an overweight aircraft. He had calculated that he needed at least 400 gallons of fuel to reach Paris, but after a test flight with only 300 gallons it was found that the undercarriage was buckling and tyre wear excessive. This ruled out any further test flights. Nonetheless Lindbergh decided that the runway at Roosevelt airfield should be long enough for a take-off with a full fuel-load, and some sources say he ended up carrying as much as 450 gallons of fuel.

Lindbergh was almost ready to depart. His plan was to prepare the aircraft in privacy and partly fill the tanks at Curtiss airfield, then fly to the adjacent Roosevelt airfield where Byrd had generously allowed him to use the extra long runway. At 3 a.m. on 20 May, however, the weather was too bad to make the flight to Roosevelt and the aircraft had to go by road. In great secrecy auxiliary wheels were fitted to its tail and it was hitched up to a lorry. It was then carefully towed over rough, unmade back roads to Roosevelt airfield.

Lindbergh stopped on the way and bought five chicken sandwiches. Asked whether they would be sufficient for his flight, he said 'If I get to Paris, I won't need any more, and if I don't get to Paris I won't need any more either'. In spite of atrocious weather, with reports of worse to come, Lindbergh decided to go.

LINDBERGH

One of the many souvenir postcards published to celebrate Lindbergh's flight.

Even at the last minute there was drama. Lindbergh's mechanics, Kenneth Boedecker and Ed Mulligan, found the main tank would take another 100 lbs of fuel. Torn between the example of Fonck, whose overweight aircraft had failed to take off, and Nungesser and Coli, who may have lived if they had carried extra fuel, Lindbergh decided to take it.

When the engine was given its final test it was found to be slightly down on power. This would not normally have been a concern, but with the aircraft overloaded Lindbergh wanted all the power he could get. A further disadvantage was the 5 m.p.h. tail wind (a head wind would have provided more lift), but despite these problems Lindbergh pressed ahead and was away at 7.52 a.m. on 20 May 1927.

The soft, muddy runway held him back and he built up speed very slowly. To make matters worse, he daren't let the tail rise for fear the aircraft would pitch forward, smashing the propellor. This caused the tail skid to sink into the ground and slow him even more. Two onlookers, stationed at the point where he had hoped to leave the ground, claimed that they could clearly see him, his face white and strained. At the last possible moment Lindbergh dragged his plane into the air, as if by sheer willpower. He missed a tractor by ten feet and power lines by twenty.

For the next 37 hours Charles Lindbergh fought two battles. The rain, cloud banks, fog and ice were bad enough, but his greatest enemy was sleep. Although he had trained himself to stay awake for over 40 hours, the trauma and excitement of his departure meant that he had not slept for 63 hours by the time he finally arrived in Paris. He said later that he was kept awake by the instability of his plane. If he dozed off, it tried to fall out of the sky. At 10.24 p.m. local time on 21 May 1927, Lindbergh touched down at Le Bourget airport to a tumultuous welcome, only three miles off-course after flying 3,600 miles in 33 hours.

This plaque is believed to have been unveiled at Le Bourget airport, although in fact Lindbergh landed there on 21 May, not 22 May.

CHARLES LINDBERGH
APRÈS AVOIR TRAVERSÉ
L'ATLANTIQUE
ATTERRIT ICI LE 22 MAI 1927

LIGUE INTERNATIONALE
DES AVIATEURS. PRÉSIDENT:
C.B. HARMON

LES VIEILLES TIGES
. PRÉSIDENT:
LÉON BATHIAT

C·A·LINDBERGH
Traversée de l'Atlantique, 20–21 Mai 1927.

A dazed Lindbergh in Paris.

DIX
PARIS

OUR HERO
CHAS. A. LINDBERGH

NEW YORK   PARIS

MAY 21. 1927

Mobbed by 160,000 people, Lindbergh was dragged from the plane and carried aloft for over half an hour before being rescued. According to one report, the American ambassador and official reception committee were seeking refuge from the mob in a pavilion when a window suddenly flew open and a young blond man was bundled through. 'I'm not Lindbergh, my name's Harry Wheeler', he cried. According to Wheeler, somebody had jammed a flying helmet similar to Lindbergh's on his head, possibly in an attempt to confuse the crowd.

Eventually Lindbergh reached the American embassy and safety, and was later received by the French President and awarded the Cross of the Legion of Honour. To save weight, he had left personal belongings including spare clothing behind in America. The borrowed suit that he is wearing in the ceremonial pictures is said to have belonged to a friend of the American ambassador's valet.

America went wild when the news broke that he had made it. Before the flight newspapers had described him as 'the flying fool', but within hours his image changed to 'Lindbergh, our hero'. Almost as fast was his promotion from lieutenant in the Army Reserve Corps to captain. Then the money began to roll in. Within a week he had offers totalling more than $5 million for exclusive rights to his story.

Lindbergh being received in Brussels.

After a hectic week of ceremonies, presentations and yet more medals, Lindbergh left Paris. Circling the Eiffel Tower twice, watched by hundreds of thousands of people, he flew to Brussels to meet King Albert of Belgium and then continued on to Croydon. From Dover onwards Lindbergh insisted on flying at treetop height, accompanied according to one source by a 'veritable circus' of aircraft.

An estimated crowd of 120,000 broke down barriers and stampeded onto the aerodrome at Croydon. Lindbergh had to abort his first attempt at landing, and only just avoided causing injury to the crowds on his second attempt. Other pilots, desperately short of fuel, had problems finding landing spaces elsewhere. According to one report the crowd got out of control and the aircraft was damaged by the crush. Lindbergh was at last rescued and taken to the airport control tower, but not before having to fight off a man who tried to snatch his helmet. To escape from the frenzied mob he had to make a flying leap from the control tower ladder to the American ambassador's car. He then became the first celebrity to be welcomed at the present Croydon airport terminal building.

Crowds greeting Lindbergh at Croydon airport.

Lindbergh at Croydon.

He got the greatest fright of his life whilst being taken to London by car. 'A large limousine drove right at us on the wrong side of the road and our chauffeur seemed to be driving straight at it. When I opened my eyes it was gone. Nobody told me they drive on the left in England.' During his time in London he was received by King George V and Queen Mary at Buckingham Palace. He also met the Prince of Wales (later Edward VII) and Princess Elizabeth (our present Queen). Other receptions followed at both the House of Commons and the House of Lords. At a reception in his honour at the prestigious Savoy Hotel, five chicken sandwiches were set before him. Amidst laughter and applause the Master of Ceremonies announced 'Captain Lindbergh will now partake of his customary meal'!

Lindbergh had originally planned to continue from Croydon on a triumphant tour around the world, but the American ambassador to Great Britain, Alanson B. Houghton, opposed this. Lindbergh described his aircraft as a beloved companion, and said he wouldn't permit it to be shipped home 'in a coffin', although in the end he bowed to pressure and returned to America on the battleship that was waiting for him. Plans for gigantic receptions were well underway in Washington, New York and St Louis – America was not going to permit Europe to outdo her in welcoming home her hero.

Policemen watch over the *Spirit of St Louis*.

Having received a tumultuous welcome wherever he went, Lindbergh left Croydon in great secrecy early on the morning of 31 May. His destination was Gosport, where the *Spirit of St Louis* was dismantled and packed in two crates. Afterwards these were taken by rail to Southampton and loaded on board the battleship *Memphis*. Years later, one of the crates was found and after restoration became a small museum.

And now it's back once again to the chicken sandwiches. In the early 1990s I met Arthur Freeman, the airman standing on the left of the picture of *Spirit of St Louis* at Gosport (facing page). He was twenty at the time and spent the night on guard duty in the cockpit. Two of Lindbergh's sandwiches were still there!

The RAF lent Lindbergh a Hawker fighter to return to RAF Kenley, and he insisted on performing aerobatics on the way. He stayed overnight at Kenley before flying to France in another borrowed fighter to join the *Memphis*.

Spirit of St Louis at Gosport.

On his arrival in Washington on Saturday 11 June 1927, Lindbergh was welcomed by an armada of ships while scores of aircraft circled overhead. A fifteen-gun salute in honour of the admiral commanding the *Memphis* was followed by another for Lindbergh of twenty-one guns, normally only given to presidents and foreign heads of state. Charles Lindbergh and his mother were hurried away in an open car and were officially welcomed by President Coolidge at the Washington Memorial, where the President awarded Lindbergh the Distinguished Flying Cross. On the Monday morning he flew himself to New York, where following a reception on the Mayor of New York's yacht, *Macon*, there was a ticker tape procession through the city. Following several days of celebrations in New York Lindbergh was presented with the $25,000 prize by Raymond Orteig. On the Thursday he flew back to Washington, and on the Friday continued to St Louis for an official reception there.

'New York. Amazing scenes at home-coming of Lindbergh.'

A month after his triumphant return to the United States, Lindbergh set off on another adventure, a victory tour throughout the country lasting three months. In all he made 81 landings, visiting all 48 states, with each landing scheduled for exactly 2 p.m. He also dropped greetings messages at over 190 other locations. At the end of the year he embarked on what became known as his Pan-American tour. This led him across the United States and down through Mexico into South America as far as Columbia and Venezuela. He returned to St Louis via the Caribbean and Cuba.

Lindbergh's reception in the Canal Zone during his Pan-American tour.

Spirit of St Louis was presented to the Smithsonian Museum in Washington where it remains to this day. It was initially displayed in the Arts and Industries building, and it is said that over the years Lindbergh made several private visits to the museum to see the aircraft in which he had flown over 40,000 miles. Years later, an exact replica was built for the film *Spirit of St Louis*, starring Jimmy Stewart as the 25-year-old Lindbergh. On test flights it was assessed as being almost unflyable. In desperation they asked Lindbergh's opinion. After an hour's flight he reported that he had forgotten just what a joy it was to fly!

Spirit of St Louis **as originally displayed in the Smithsonian Museum.**

Meanwhile, what of Chamberlin and Levine? Following news that Lindbergh had been seen over Ireland on 21 May, Chamberlin moved *Columbia* to Roosevelt airfield for take-off, but on arrival there was stopped by police as he had no written permit to use the runway. He ordered *Columbia* to be put back in the hangar, but as the aircraft was overloaded it got stuck in mud and some of its fuel had to be dumped on the ground to lighten the load. When a careless bystander dropped a lighted cigarette the ground around the aircraft burst into flames, although it was fortunately rolled clear without damage.

On 4 June, about two weeks after this fiasco, Clarence Chamberlin was sitting in the cockpit of *Columbia* waiting to take off for Europe, and according to Levine the navigator was on his way. Levine was accompanied by his wife, which made a change as he was usually seen with an actress named Mabel Boll, known as the Queen of Diamonds after her ostentatious gem display. It was said

that the huge diamonds were paste, except when Levine was around. To everyone's surprise – especially, some say, Chamberlin's – Levine joined him in the aircraft and away they went. His wife fainted from shock. Later his attorney gave her a note saying goodbye. Their destination was initially unclear, although a telegraph addressed to Chamberlin was discovered later and revealed they were heading for Berlin.

It was not long before Chamberlin discovered that Levine was completely useless as a navigator and they were lost. By good fortune, they came across the liner *Mauretania* heading for New York. From the direction in which she had come and her departure date, obtained from a newspaper, they worked out where to head next and roughly how far they had to go. Eventually they found themselves over France. Steering more by guess and God than science, they set a vague course for Berlin. Just before they arrived, their luck and fuel ran out.

The *Mauretania*, which acted as a marker for Chamberlin and Levine.

Chamberlin and Levine in Germany
after their long flight.

Chamberlin der Oceanflieger

Chamberlins Flugzeug
„COLUMBIA"

Levine sein Begleiter

Their journey ended in a field only 30 miles from Berlin after a world-record flight of 3,911 miles in 42 hours and 45 minutes (slightly longer flights had been made previously, but these were 'closed circuit' – i.e. flown in circles over land and hence in much less difficult circumstances). Villagers gave them 30 gallons of fuel in exchange for $5, also lending them an old teapot as they had no other way of refilling their tank. When asked the way to Berlin the villagers waved their arms in several directions. So once again they took off and hoped for the best. They were still arguing violently when they ran out of fuel again. This time they were not so lucky. They crash-landed, and although they were not hurt the aircraft's propellor and fuselage were damaged.

Eventually they reached Berlin to a heroes' welcome. However, as Levine had been beaten by Lindbergh on the New York to Paris flight, he wanted to eclipse his rival by making the more difficult direct flight from Paris to New York. Chamberlin was not enthusiastic and eventually went home by sea. Recalling the flight with Levine, he said that the worst moment came after he had spent over 30 continuous hours at the controls. On trying to get some sleep, he was awakened by the plane falling out of the sky in a stall. Levine, who was piloting the aircraft, seemed to find this very amusing. They fell about 17,000 feet before Chamberlin regained control.

Crowds greeting Chamberlin and Levine in Berlin.

Enthusiastischer Empfang der Ozeanflieger Chamberlin und Levine auf dem Berliner Flughafen.

Levine and Drouhin alongside *Columbia*.

Edit. Farineau

The next person to get involved with Levine was French ace pilot Maurice Drouhin, who Levine planned to make the non-stop flight from Paris to New York with. However, true to form, he was soon having endless arguments with Drouhin. As a result of one violent row, Levine emptied *Columbia*'s fuel tanks to stop Drouhin flying to America without him. Drouhin then put guards around the aircraft to stop Levine employing another pilot for the flight. In a rage, Levine bribed the guards to let him carry out some taxi tests and promptly took off from Paris, bound for Croydon, on 29 August 1927. The authorities were horrified. Levine, with very limited experience and having never flown alone, was attempting to fly through the most congested airspace in Europe. He had no maps and only a vague idea that Croydon was 'somewhere to the north'.

At Croydon there was absolute pandemonium. Emergency services were mobilised and passengers were kept in the terminal building in case something very nasty happened. According to contemporary reports Levine came in about 50 feet too high, stalled, then struggled up to a safe height, only just missing a hangar roof. His second approach was just as bad. In desperation, a local pilot flew alongside him to guide him down. This time the landing was too fast and too hard. However, the aircraft rolled to a stop after a series of 30-foot bounces.

Croydon airport around the time of Levine's landing.

Columbia was taken home by sea, but flew the Atlantic again in 1930. This time J. Errol Boyd and Harry Connor were trying to make the first non-stop flight from Canada to England. They took off from Montreal on 20 September but were forced to land at Prince Edward Island because of bad weather, eventually reaching Harbour Grace, Newfoundland. Taking off from there on 9 October, they reached Croydon two days later after being forced down at Tresco, Isles of Scilly. *Columbia*, however, proved itself to be safe and reliable by being the first aeroplane to fly the Atlantic twice.

Ironically, Levine may have contributed to the deaths of both Bertaud and Drouhin by denying them an Atlantic flight in *Columbia*. Both died with several companions in flights using inferior aircraft. Bertaud and two companions were lost at sea in September 1927 along with their Fokker FVII. Maurice Drouhin was killed, together with his mechanic, on a test flight in a Couzinet aircraft on 8 August 1928.

Maurice Drouhin with a Farman aircraft, also intended for a transatlantic flight.

DROUHIN
et son Avion Transatlantique *"FARMAN"*

In June 1927 Commander Byrd was ready to attempt an Atlantic flight from the United States to Paris, although by this time there was no particular sense of urgency as Lindbergh had already achieved this milestone. To overcome the usual problem of getting a vastly overloaded plane into the air his aircraft, the *America*, was hauled up a specially constructed ramp fifteen feet high and the tail tied up to a stake. Wheel brakes had yet to be invented and the idea was that the securing rope should be cut with an axe when the engines developed full power. There was controversy about whether this could be achieved before the tail was pulled off. In fact the problem solved itself when the rope broke and the huge aircraft lumbered down the ramp, along the runway and into the air. There were four men on board: pilots Bert Acosta and Bernt Balchen sat in the front cockpit, along with mechanic George Noville. Richard Byrd sat on his own in a cockpit behind them, with the only means of communication being shouting or passing notes. After the point of no return, Byrd was dismayed to be told by his fellow crew-members that excessive fuel consumption meant that they could not reach land, although they had no option but to carry onwards.

COMMANDER BYRD flew from Spitzenbergen to the North Pole and back in approximately 15 hours, May 9, 1926.

Byrd and the *America*.

Several hours later he was informed that a mistake had been made and they could at least reach Ireland. Those on board got another fright when it became apparent that Bert Acosta (the pilot who had previously been involved with Levine) had very limited blind flying experience. At one point they found themselves diving uncontrollably earthwards at 160 m.p.h. With great skill the other pilot, Bernt Balchen, saved the aircraft and from then on did all the blind flying. After many hours in storm clouds and fog they found themselves over the coast of France. They were 250 miles off-course and had missed Ireland altogether. Their earth inductor compass, with which Lindbergh had reached France only three miles adrift, failed because it had not been oiled, and their other compasses both pointed in different directions. The source of error was possibly static electricity or the fact that the compasses were positioned close to a stack of steel petrol drums. As the radio operator emptied fuel into the main petrol tank and threw the empty drums over the side, the compasses were affected by the resulting changes in magnetic field.

One of the pilots suggested following the railway lines to Paris but Byrd wanted to find the mouth of the Seine, using that as a guide instead. After several hours in cloud and fog so thick that they couldn't see their wing tips he had to acknowledge that they were lost (although unbeknown to them their engines had been heard over Paris). After some time, with fuel running low, they were very relieved to see a light. Their relief turned to horror when they realised it was a lighthouse and that they were heading out to sea. Their only option was to crash-land near the shore. After 43 hours' flight time, the *Atlantic* landed safely in ten feet of water and it was not long before the crew were rescued. The location was Ver-sur-Mer, later to become famous as Omaha Beach on D-Day, 6 June 1944. The following day they were disconsolate to find that their aircraft had been stripped by souvenir hunters. To add insult to injury, by the time the official mail, recovered with great care, reached Paris, all the stamps had been removed from the letters. They were on sale on the black market at $10 each as collectors' items.

Richard Byrd, photographed on the SS *Macon* in New York after one of his record-breaking flights.

The *America* after its crash landing.

The *Pride of Detroit*.

Lieut. Col. F. F. Minchin, who was lost with the *St Raphael*.

F. F. Minchin

Following Lindbergh's non-stop flight from the US to Paris, other aviators began to consider more daring record-breaking flights. William Brock and Edward Schlee left Newfoundland in August 1927 in a Stinson, *Pride of Detriot*, with the target of completing a round the world flight in fifteen days. On reaching land the first indication of their position was the word 'Dawlish' painted on a station roof (in the UK at that time place names were painted on station roofs as an aid to pilots). They were over England, and from that point followed railway lines to Croydon. This was the first direct Atlantic flight by an aeroplane to have reached the British mainland. From Croydon they flew to Japan, clocking up 18,410 miles in 191 flying hours from their starting point in Detroit. They arrived in Tokyo on 12 September where they were arrested for flying over military installations. Their plane was seized and they returned to America by sea.

Unfortunately, most of the other attempts to fly the Atlantic in the year following Lindbergh's achievement failed. In all, nineteen aircraft took off across the ocean and only five achieved their goal. Thirteen airmen were lost at sea. In the summer of 1927 Lieutenant Colonel Frederick F. Minchin and Captain Leslie Hamilton, along with their passenger, Princess Lowenstein-Wertheim, disappeared without trace. The 62-year-old princess, the daughter of the Earl of Mexborough, had financed the flight. On 31 August 1927 they took off from the RAF base at Upavon, Wiltshire, bound for Ottawa. Their aircraft, a single-engined Fokker FVIIa, *St Raphael*, had been blessed by the Roman Catholic Archbishop of Cardiff. The princess was seated in a wicker chair in the rear cockpit with two attaché cases, a picnic basket containing bottles of red wine, and two red hatboxes at her side. The heavily-laden aircraft had great difficulty getting airborne, requiring every foot of the mile-long runway, and the journey was made more difficult because of the adverse winds encountered when travelling east to west. *St Raphael* was identified by a ship when halfway across the Atlantic but never made landfall. No trace of the aircraft or its crew was ever found.

Ruth Elder, a New York showgirl and small-time actress, had ambitions to become the first woman to fly from the United States to Europe. She hoped to gain publicity, and for this reason called her Stinson monoplane *American Girl*. With George Haldeman as pilot, *American Girl* left New York on 11 October 1927.

Haldeman and Elder's experience illustrates how easily the crews of other flights and their aircraft could disappear without trace. After many hours in the air an oil pipe broke and *American Girl* was forced to land on the sea. By this time, possibly through ignorance of wind velocity and direction, they were far to the south of their intended route, near the Azores and heading for Africa. They had covered sufficient miles to have reached England if they had stayed on course. Fortunately their SOS was heard, and they were picked up by a liner (this was possibly the first rescue from an aircraft due to an SOS message). A showgirl to the last, Ruth Elder is reported to have refused to leave the rapidly sinking aircraft until she had repaired her make-up. Later, Elder made her name as a very successful short circuit air racing pilot.

Ruth Elder.

RUTH ELDER holds world's cross country race for women, Santa Monica, Cal., to Cleveland, Ohio and return in her plane, "American Girl."

© 1930 EXHIBIT SUPPLY CO., CHICAGO

This dramatic photograph shows the _Bremen_ struggling to get into the air after the point by which it should have taken off.

The _Bremen_ and her crew.

In spite of several attempts, by mid-1927 no aircraft had conquered the Atlantic from east to west, flying against the prevailing winds. On 14 August that year, two identical Junkers F33 aircraft took off from Berlin bound for New York. The Junkers F33 was a very advanced aircraft for its time. Of all-metal construction and with an enclosed cockpit, it was very efficient aerodynamically but extremely underpowered. For political reasons, Germany was only allowed to produce aircraft engines with very low power output at the time. The _Bremen_ began the journey, while _Europa_ turned back with engine trouble. Herman Koehl, Baron Gunther von Huenefeld and Frederick Loose flew on in the _Bremen_, battling against strong headwinds over England and Ireland and out over the Atlantic. They soon realised that with their land speed limited to less than 60 m.p.h. they had no chance of reaching land before their fuel ran out. Wisely, they headed for home. To give their aircraft a good proving flight they returned to Berlin via Hull, Dover and Calais, a distance of 1,800 miles.

The following year Koehl and von Huenefeld decided on a shorter route, starting from Ireland. This time the third crew member was Commandant James Fitzmaurice of the Irish Free State Air Force. Leaving Baldonnel on 12 April 1928 they battled on against the headwinds, generally flying only 100 feet above the sea but still unable to maintain even 60 m.p.h. A broken fuel line, cockpit lighting failure and other problems meant that Koehl and Fitzmaurice were only able to pilot the plane for about an hour at a time. With more than 400 miles to go to America, they became completely lost in thick fog. By then they had been in the air for two days and a night. Eventually, after about twelve hours of battling against fog, snow and icing problems, lost and nearly out of fuel, they came upon an island with a lighthouse. This turned out to be Greenley Island, just off Labrador. Koehl made a valiant attempt at a landing but the snow and ice proved too much. The undercarriage collapsed, and the propellor was also smashed.

After the crew of the _Bremen_ reached safety at the lighthouse, several attempts were made to rescue them and their aircraft. Von Huenefeld, Koehl and Fitzmaurice were eventually flown to New York and later given a triumphant reception in Berlin. The _Bremen_ was recovered and put on show at the Henry Ford Museum, Detroit. One of the pilots who took part in the rescue attempt was Floyd Bennett, who had been a member of Richard Byrd's crew on his polar flight. Bennett had been injured when they had crashed during Byrd's test flight, and had not recovered fully from this crash. He was taken ill during the rescue attempt and later died.

Köhl Fitzmaurice v. Hünefeld

The crew of the *Bremen* were fêted in Berlin.

Einzug der Ozean-Flieger in Berlin am 20. Juni, 1928.

AÉRODROME DU BOURGET-DUGNY

ASSOLLANT LEFÈVRE LOTTI SCHREIBER

This postcard, showing the stowaway Schreiber alongside the crew of *L'Oiseau Canari*, is very rare compared with the alternative illustrating just the crew.

By 1928, the deaths of airmen such as Noel Davis and Stanton Wooster meant that aviators were beginning to get the message that it was not a good idea to take off in overloaded aircraft without carrying out test flights. Three Frenchmen, Jean Assollant, Rene Lefèvre and Armand Lotti were confident that their aircraft, *L'Oiseau Canari*, had been thoroughly tested and had more than enough power to get them off the ground and to France without any problems. However, their take-off from a beach in Maine, USA seemed certain to end in disaster. They just could not get the tail to lift. After nearly a mile they just managed to scrape over a sea wall at the very end of the beach. It was obvious that there was something drastically wrong with their aircraft. Unfortunately, with a full load of petrol they were far too heavy for an emergency landing. Their only option was to throw overboard as much of their equipment as possible and hope for the best. Just as Armand Lotti was frantically unbolting the radio, a stowaway appeared from a compartment near the tail of the aircraft. He calmly introduced himself as a journalist named Arthur Schreiber. Without his weight in the tail, the aircraft flew perfectly again, and in spite of thunderstorms, rain and fog they eventually made landfall near Santander, Spain (they were well off-course due to the effects of a magnetic storm which had upset their main compass). Apparently, after their initial impulse to throw Schreiber overboard, they showed him no ill will. A mascot called Rufus, a small crocodile, was the fifth crew-member.

Charles Kingsford Smith alongside the *Southern Cross*.

After the *Bremen*'s success in April 1928 it was to be two years before the next east to west flight. In this case the journey was to be the penultimate stage in the first round the world flight to include a crossing of the equator. Pilot Charles Kingsford Smith (later Sir Charles) had already flown many thousands of miles from west coast America to Australia and on to England (crew members differed on the different legs of the journey). Kingsford Smith had joined the Australian Army at the start of the First World War, serving as a dispatch rider before joining the British Royal Flying Corps and eventually becoming a pilot and winning the Military Cross for bravery. After the war he became a stunt pilot in Hollywood. Prevented from making a transpacific flight home, he returned to Australia by sea and made a reputation in air racing. With financial help he purchased a Fokker aircraft from Sir Hubert Wilkins, a famous Arctic explorer. He named it the *Southern Cross*.

The *Southern Cross* was a hybrid machine constructed from the parts of two different Fokker aircraft. One feature of its design was that the huge main fuel tank could be emptied in seconds if the crew were forced to land on water. The giant wooden wing and fuselage would hopefully keep them afloat for several hours. In 1929 the *Southern Cross* broke existing records by flying from Sydney to London in under thirteen days. The chosen take-off point for the flight to New York was the concrete-like sands of Portmarnock Strand near Dublin. The estimated time for the flight was 35 hours, giving the crew only two hours' reserves of fuel. Seen off by a crowd of 5,000 people who had waited up most of the night, they departed on 24 June 1930 and made good progress at first, although adverse winds limited their ground speed to about 80 m.p.h. Unlike previous Atlantic flights they were able to maintain radio contact with shipping most of the time. This was fortunate as towards the end of their flight, probably due to static electricity, their two magnetic compasses gave wildly inaccurate readings. Instead, they were able to rely on radio bearings for navigation. Unfortunately, due to adverse winds, it became apparent that they could not reach New York and they landed at Harbour Grace, Newfoundland, before completing their journey the next day. The *Southern Cross* was the first aircraft to land in New York after a flight from Europe.

The *Southern Cross*.

Costes, Bellonte and *Point d'Interrogation*.

Following Lindbergh's flight from New York to Paris, there was great pressure on French aviators to make a non-stop flight in the other direction. On 13 July 1929 Dieudonne Costes and Maurice Bellonte took off from Paris in their Breguet *Point d'Interrogation* (Question Mark). Costes was well known as a former pilot on the Air Union Croydon to Paris route, and for long-distance flights from Paris to Siberia, Persia and South America, among others. Bellonte acted as mechanic, radio operator and navigator. Their aircraft was well-equipped with a radio set, ample room for provisions, a dinghy and parachutes. However, this attempt ended in failure, with high fuel consumption and adverse weather conditions forcing them to return to Paris.

In order to prove that their aircraft had adequate range before making a second Atlantic attempt, Costes and Bellonte set another record by completing a 4,913 mile flight from Paris to Manchuria in 51 hours (leaving Paris on 27 September 1929). In September 1930 they successfully flew the Atlantic, reaching New York in 37 hours after a flight of 3,700 miles. Bellonte's great skill as a navigator and weather reports from shipping along the route played a major part in their success. Lindbergh and 25,000 spectators greeted them with a rapturous ticker tape welcome in New York. They then set out on a 16,000 mile flying tour of major American cities. In 1980, fifty years after his record-breaking flight, Maurice Bellonte made another Atlantic flight from Paris to New York. This time he went by Concorde.

On one occasion Costes and Bellonte flew to Croydon on the famous *Rayon d'Or* and were welcomed by Amy Johnson. Between 1929 and 1933 the French airline Air Union operated a fleet of thirteen Loiré et Olivier LeO 213 airliners on the routes from Paris to London, Marseilles and Geneva. These had *Rayon d'Or* painted on the starboard side and the English translation *Golden Ray* on the port side (some people thought they were different aircraft). This was a luxury service and the aircraft each carried twelve passengers in restaurant-style surroundings designed by Compagnie des Wagon-Lits, complete with bar and barman.

Costes, Bellonte and Amy Johnson.

Londres. — *Costes et Bellonte, les as de l'Atlantique, serrent la main de la célèbre aviatrice anglaise Miss Anny Johnson.*
Londen. — *Costes en Bellonte, de overwinnaars van den Atlantischen Oceaan, drukken de hand der gekende engelsche vliegster, Miss Anny Johnson.*

In 1916, plans were afoot in Germany to create the largest aircraft in the world. Several years before the first Atlantic flight, this was intended to not only cross the Atlantic, but carry passengers too. The Dornier Do X was the brainchild of Professor Claude Dornier (1884–1969). It was named Do X temporarily to signify that it was an unknown quantity, but later the name was retained officially.

The giant hulk of the Do X.

Das Dornier Flugschiff Do X mit 12 Motoren à 500 Ps. wird zu Wasser gebr

This view of the flight deck gives a good impression of the Do X's massive construction.

Despite being conceived in 1916, it was many years before the Do X was actually built and ready to make an Atlantic attempt. It did, however, show great promise, demonstrating its load-carrying capacity on 21 October 1929 when it completed a one hour flight with 169 people on board, including nine stowaways. At a time when airliners that could carry more than twenty passengers were rare, the Do X was designed to take 72. They had the luxury of a bar, lounge, sleeping quarters, smoking- and writing rooms, all arranged over three decks.

In addition to the flight deck, the massive Do X had a separate control room for its twelve engines. At first Siemens radial engines were fitted, but due to overheating problems these were replaced by very advanced liquid-cooled Curtiss V12s. Unfortunately at the same time it was found necessary to replace the streamlined sub wing supporting the original engines by a series of struts. This reduced the effective wing lifting area by nearly 350 square feet. Thus in spite of an increase in power, the aircraft was still underpowered and was unable to struggle up to an altitude of more than 1,200 feet.

The Do X had six pairs of engines mounted on its wings.

The Do X reached New York on 27 August 1931.

On 2 November 1930, with the designer himself on board, the Dornier Do X left Germany on a demonstration flight to South America and the United States. The route was by way of Amsterdam, Southampton, Bordeaux, Lisbon, the Canary Islands, Fernando de Noronha, Natal, Rio, Antigua, Miami and so to New York. Unfortunately, the flight was something of a disaster. Part of a wing was destroyed in an engine fire at Lisbon and had to be replaced, and the hull was damaged when taking off from the Canaries. There were also various delays due to mechanical problems and bad weather. Reliability was very poor. Due to the weight of the 3,500 gallons of fuel on board (probably more than had been carried on test flights), the aircraft could not struggle up to a height of more than 60 feet at times. There is an unconfirmed report that, in the heat of the tropics, it was unable to take off at all on one occasion and spare parts

and supplies had to be sent to the next destination by ship to reduce the load. The Do X eventually reached New York on 27 August 1931.

On the return journey in 1932 the Do X fared better, the flight from Newfoundland to Plymouth taking about three days. Due to high fuel consumption, refuelling stops had to be made at destinations including Horta, Azores and Virgo, Spain. Although ahead of its time in many ways, the Do X was impractical and required a vast amount of further development. It was put on display in a museum in Germany where it was destroyed by bombing during the war. Two further aircraft were built for Italy. These had Fiat engines and were intended for use in the Mediterranean. However, mainly due to the world Depression of the 1930s, they were never put into service and were eventually broken up.

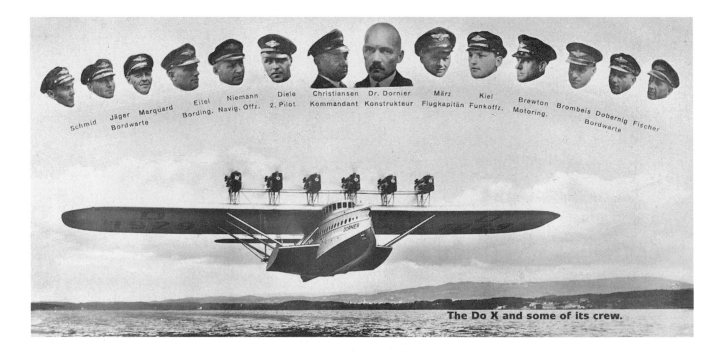

The Do X and some of its crew.

This rare postcard of Boardman and Polando was carried on the *Cape Cod* and posted from Istanbul by Russell Boardman.

At 10 a.m. on 28 July 1931, Russell Boardman and John Polando took off from Floyd Bennett airfield, New York, in a Bellanca monoplane called *Cape Cod*. They flew direct to Istanbul, Turkey, in 50 hours and 8 minutes, a journey of 5,011.8 miles. On the way they dropped a copy of the *New York Times* on Le Bourget airport in Paris. This flight broke the existing long distance record of Costes and Bellonte (4,913 miles from Paris to Manchuria). Their route from the USA to Turkey was via France, Switzerland, Italy, Yugoslavia, Greece and Bulgaria.

On the same day, at 10.17 a.m., Hugh Herndon and Clyde Pangborn took off from Floyd Bennett airfield in a Bellanca called *Miss Veedol*. Although aiming to fly non-stop to Moscow, they decided to land en route in the UK because of stormy weather, touching down near Moylgrove, Pembrokeshire. They apparently turned up at the Black Lion Inn, explained that they had just flown in from New York, and requested a meal and a room for the night. Their journey continued over Berlin, Moscow, across Russia and Siberia, and they reached Japan on 5 August. There they were arrested and jailed for spying, not having a landing permit. They were not released until October when a $1,000 fine was paid.

Hugh Herndon and Clyde Pangborn standing alongside *Miss Veedol*.

Miss Veedol didn't appear to suffer extensive damage when she landed on her belly at Wenatchee.

To reduce the weight of their aircraft and thereby fit an extra fuel tank, Herndon and Pangborn redesigned the undercarriage so that it could be jettisoned after take-off. The Japanese authorities granted them permission to make only one attempt at take-off – if this failed they would have to go home by sea. They successfully got off the ground and flew non-stop from Japan to Wenatchee, Washington state, roughly following a route over the Aleutian Islands and Alaska. This was the first flight from Japan to America and the 4,727 mile journey took 41 hours. With a different crew of three, and renamed *American Nurse*, the same aircraft was subsequently lost over the Atlantic.

Wiley Post and Harold Gatty alongside *Winnie Mae*.

In the years after the First World War conflict erupted in Hungary, which underwent a revolution and saw the loss of two thirds of its territory to neighbouring states. To focus attention on their country's plight and gain publicity it was decided that Hungarian aviators should attempt an Atlantic flight. Funds for the flight were raised both in Hungary and by emigrants in America. The main impetus came from the Hungarian Church and newspapers, as well as ex-members of the Hungarian Air Force. Lord Rothermere, owner of the *Daily Mail*, offered a prize of $10,000 to the first pilot to make a non-stop flight from the North American continent to Budapest.

The front and reverse of a postcard sold for $1 to raise money for Endresz and Magyar's flight to Hungary and carried on the flight.

Opposite: By mid-1931, interest had waned in Atlantic crossings unless they were part of a longer flight. Wiley Post and Harold Gatty attracted great attention as their flight was the first stage in a journey round the world. Post despised life as a farmer's son in Kansas and longed to be a pilot. He had seen an aircraft for the first time at a county fair in 1913. After studying at a car repair school in Kansas City and a government-sponsored radio school he became an engineer at an oilfield. With insurance compensation for the loss of an eye in a drilling accident, he bought an old aeroplane and learnt to fly. In 1931 he was offered the chance to attempt a flight round the world by a rich oilman to whom he was personal pilot. He and Gatty left Roosevelt airfield on 23 June and after a very fast crossing to England in their Lockheed Vega – christened *Winnie Mae* after the owner's daughter – continued round the world in under nine days, less than five of which were made up of actual flying time. On 15 July 1933, again in *Winnie Mae* but this time solo, Post set off round the world again, bettering his first attempt by 21 hours. On the first leg of the journey he flew direct to Berlin, making the first non-stop flight from New York.

**Gyorgy Endresz, Sandor Magyar and *Justice for Hungary*.
This postcard was carried on the flight.**

**A postcard featuring *Justice for Hungary*
promoting the 1932 flight. Part of the text may
have been blacked out following Endresz's death.**

Gyorgy Endresz and Sandor Magyar left New York for Budapest in *Justice for Hungary* on 13 July 1931 and flew to Harbour Grace, Newfoundland. They were delayed by bad weather but continued their journey late on 15 July. Their aircraft was heavily overloaded, and on take-off from Harbour Grace they nearly came to grief on rocks and trees at the end of the runway. However, they made good progress and crossed the ocean in about thirteen hours. Within 30 miles of Budapest, where a crowd said to number 180,000 was waiting for them at Matyasfold aerodrome, the engine of *Justice for Hungary* misfired, short of fuel. Unable to make his pilot hear his shouted instructions, Magyar frantically wrote him a note telling him to change tanks. It was too late, the engine stopped, and they had to make a crash landing. Although they were not hurt, their aircraft was too badly damaged to continue. They had over 100 litres of fuel left in the tanks, more than enough to have reached Budapest. Lord Rothermere still awarded them the $10,000 prize.

After the flight, Alexander Magyar reverted to his real name of Wilczek (Magyar, meaning 'Hungarian', had been adopted by Wilczek for the flight). He and Endresz fell out about how the proceeds from the sale of the aircraft should be divided, and a duel was scheduled for 26 October, although this was called off at the last minute. The following day Wilczek married the former wife of his fencing master, and eventually returned to America. Endresz retained control of *Justice for Hungary* and in May 1932 took off from Budapest for Rome for the Congress of International Fliers organised by General Balbo. He crashed on landing, killing both himself and his radio operator.

Two years later, prompted by similar motives to those of Endresz and Magyar, two Lithuanian Air Force officers, Captain Stephen Darius and Lieutenant Stanley Girenas, planned to fly from New York to Kovno, Lithuania, to draw attention to their country's oppression. They were refused permission for their flight because their Bellanca, *Lituanica*, was not equipped with a radio. They left New York in great secrecy on 15 July 1933 without authorisation. Most of the world probably didn't even know they had taken off when it was announced on 17 July that both men were dead. After successfully crossing the Atlantic, their aircraft crashed near Soldin, Germany, 400 miles from their destination.

Darius and Girenas alongside *Lituanica*.

Darius and Girenas are commemorated on this beautiful but sombre mourning card.

In memory of Darius and Girenas, Felix Waitkus attempted a similar flight in 1935. Waitkus was an American Air Force Lieutenant from Wisconsin, but of Lithuanian extraction. He took off from Floyd Bennett airfield on 21 September 1935 like others before him, and had to battle with ice, snow and fog, unable to get any bearings from sun or stars most of the time. By dawn of the second day he knew he didn't have sufficient fuel to reach Kovno. Through the fog he saw land and decided to refuel. Unfortunately, on landing in a field near Ballinrobe, Ireland, the undercarriage of *Lituanica II* collapsed. Although Waitkus was not hurt, the aircraft would take him no further. His financial backers chartered another aircraft so he could at least reach Lithuania, and *Lituanica II* was repaired and shipped home. Following Lithuania's communist take-over in 1940, the Soviet authorities took the aircraft to Moscow for evaluation.

Lituanica II.

On 20 September 1931 a steamer rescued two Germans, Willy Rody and Christian Johannsen, and their Portuguese companion Fernando Corsta Viega from the wreck of their Junkers W33, *Esa*, off Newfoundland. The aircraft was named after newly-married Willy Rody's wife, and belonged to Charles Levine. After flying from Germany to Lisbon, the three men had taken off for New York on 13 September 1931 and were forced to land at sea due to engine trouble. They were found purely by chance and were incredibly fortunate as their aircraft, which had a corrugated metal skin similar to the well-known Junkers 52, floated for seven days without breaking up. The rescue vessel was the *Belmoira*, a cargo ship bound for Leningrad from America, which sighted the *Esa* 80 miles south-west of Newfoundland.

69. — St Jean de Terre-Neuve (Atlantique). — *Les aviateurs Rodey, Johannsen et Veiga, sauvés par le vapeur « Belmoira ».*
St John New Found Land (Atlantique). — *De vliegeniers Rodey, Johannsen en Veiga, gered door het stoomschip « Belmoira ».*

The remains of the *Esa* seen from the cargo ship *Belmoira*.

Amelia Earhart.

Amelia Earhart first flew the Atlantic in 1928, and although only a passenger on that occasion (despite being a competent pilot with 500 flying hours to her credit), she was still the first woman to make the crossing. The aircraft was a Fokker seaplane, *Friendship*, and the other crew members were Commander Wilmer Stultz, US Navy and Louis Gordon, mechanic. They took off from Trepassey Bay, Newfoundland on 17 June, apparently bound for Ireland, although they missed it altogether due to fog, landing instead at Burry Port near Llanelli, Wales. Although only a passenger, some sources say Amelia Earhart was actually in command of the flight.

Popularly known as 'Lady Lindy' because of her resemblance to Charles Lindbergh, Earhart became famous for her aviation exploits. These included the first American coast-to-coast and return flight by a woman, and breaking the world altitude record for an autogiro (a sort of primitive helicopter) in 1931. In May 1932 Amelia Earhart made the first solo Atlantic flight by a woman. This flight, from Newfoundland to a Mr Gallagher's farm at Culmore, near Londonderry, was also the fastest coast-to-coast Atlantic crossing to date. Earhart and her navigator, Fred Noonan, disappeared without trace in the Pacific on an attempted round the world flight in 1937. In spite of a frantic search at the time and various subsequent expeditions to try and discover their fate, no trace of them or their aircraft has ever been found. Stories persist that they were captured by the Japanese and executed as spies.

Friendship, in which Amelia Earhart flew the Atlantic in 1928.

FRIENDSHIP U.S.A
BURRY PORT HARBOUR

Mr J. A. Mollison's light machine –
"THE HEART'S CONTENT."
5795.

**Jim Mollison and
the *Heart's
Content*.**

By 1932, an element of danger was required to arouse the public's interest in record-breaking flights, ideally combined with a touch of madness and really insane odds. Australian Jim Mollison's proposed flight was thus an ideal candidate for their attention. His plan was for a solo two-way Atlantic flight in a de Havilland Puss Moth called the *Heart's Content*. The Puss Moth was a so-called light aircraft, intended for weekend 'hops' – such as across the Channel to France. With a top speed of about 128 m.p.h. and a range of 300 miles it certainly wasn't designed for an Atlantic crossing. It also had an unenviable reputation for losing its wings, which made its choice for Mollison's planned flight even more surprising. By increasing the fuel capacity to 160 gallons, the extra load imposed on the *Heart's Content* was said to be 'equivalent to the weight of nine men, in an aeroplane designed to carry one pilot and two passengers' (*Mollison, The Flying Scotsman*). Nevertheless, Mollison had faith in his Puss Moth having broken records including flights from Australia to England and England to South Africa in similar aircraft.

Mollison took off from Portmarnock Strand near Dublin on 18 August 1932. It took nearly a mile, the whole length of the beach, before the overloaded aircraft struggled into the air. At times flying only 50 feet above the sea, he made landfall near Halifax, Nova Scotia at dawn the following day and headed for New York. Unfortunately, in blinding snow and fog, he became totally lost, and after 30 hours in the air and with only ten gallons of fuel left was forced to land. Two days later he flew on to New York where he was the talk of the town. A suite of rooms was put at his disposal at the New York Plaza, one of the city's plushest hotels, and everyone wanted to meet him including Douglas Fairbanks Junior (who offered him a role in a forthcoming film), Charles Lindbergh and Amelia Earhart. Mollison embarked on the return flight but on his way from New York to Harbour Grace ran into fog and landed at Pennfield Ridge, 30 miles south-west of St John, New Brunswick. The following day he took off to try and reach Harbour Grace but landed again at Sydney, Nova Scotia. He was diagnosed with nervous exhaustion and his wife Amy Johnson, talking to him by phone, persuaded him to return home by sea.

FLYING with BIRTHDAY GREETINGS
TO MY DEAR,
SON

*This heartfelt greeting
has been sent;
To wish for you your "Heart's Content"
This happy day!*

Mollison planned an even more ambitious journey next time. After flying from Croydon to New York, he intended to break the world long distance record by flying non-stop from there to Baghdad (5,994 miles), and then back to Britain, in all covering about 12,000 miles. His chosen aircraft was a twin-engined de Havilland Dragon named *Seafarer*. For the first time his wife Amy would be his co-pilot on a record-breaking attempt. (Amy Johnson was famous for her record-breaking flights to Australia, South Africa and Japan.) The magazines *Aeroplane* and *Flight* both doubted the couple's chances of surviving the east to west flight. Amy and Jim were very worried themselves, whilst the fact that Jim was a notoriously heavy drinker did not improve matters.

On their first attempt on 8 June 1933, the undercarriage of their overloaded aircraft collapsed as they tried to take off from Croydon airport. Neither were hurt, and those who helped them from the wreckage thought they had been lucky that the flight had ended when it did. Mollison was obviously suffering from the effects of alcohol and in no fit state to fly. Their second attempt, from Pendine Sands, Wales on 22 July 1933, also nearly finished in disaster. Flying in thick cloud, they almost crashed into cliffs on the coast of Ireland.

Seafarer after its abortive take-off from Croydon.

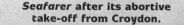

Seafarer at Pendine Sands.

On sighting land after about twenty hours, they were disappointed to find they had only averaged 87 m.p.h. Almost out of fuel, they tried to land at Bridgeport airport, 35 miles from New York. Mollison, said to be suffering from fatigue and possibly the after-effects of alcohol, made four bungled approaches. On the fifth he overshot and the aircraft crashed in a swamp behind the runway. Both he and Amy were injured.

Following hospital treatment, Mollison returned to England by sea with the remains of *Seafarer*, after souvenir-hunters had reduced the aircraft to a tattered hulk. Lord Wakefield paid for *Seafarer II* to be built, mostly using the remains of *Seafarer* (1), and Mollison brought the aircraft to Canada by sea. He and Amy Johnson attempted to take off from Wasaga Beach for Baghdad on 3 October, but crosswinds foiled two attempts at take-off and on the third the plane buckled its undercarriage. The couple decided that they were unable to beat the record flight set by Paul Codos and Maurice Rossi of 5,657 miles from New York to Rayak, Syria between 5 and 7 August 1933 and therefore abandoned their flight. A cynical editor of the *Aeroplane* took great delight in 'congratulating [Mollison] on being the first man to accompany a potentially record-breaking aeroplane on a double sea-journey across the Atlantic'.

Maurice Rossi (left) and Paul Codos, with their Bleriot 110 aircraft.

Two Canadians, Leonard Reid and James Ayling, acquired *Seafarer II* and renamed her *Trail of the Caribou*. They attempted to take up where Mollison had left off by flying non-stop to Baghdad, taking off from Wasaga Beach on 8 August 1934. After running low on fuel, they landed at Heston aerodrome outside London. Despite not having reached Baghdad, they had made the first direct flight from the Canadian mainland to England.

James Ayling, Leonard Reid and the *Trail of the Caribou*.

A Savoia–Marchetti flying boat being lowered into the sea, probably at the Orbetello seaplane base.

In December 1930 the Italian Air Force had made a successful flight to Rio de Janeiro using a squadron of Savoia–Marchetti flying boats. Following the success of this, an even greater demonstration of Italian air prowess was planned in 1933. This was to involve a 'wing' of 24 aircraft – two squadrons in all – which would fly to the Chicago Century of Progress Exposition. Leaving Orbetello, Italy on 1 July, the first stage of the journey included a flight over the Alps for which the squadron had to climb to 10,000 feet. Sadly, due to an accident at Amsterdam in which one airman was drowned, a reserve aircraft had to be deployed for the remainder of their flight. From Amsterdam they flew via Ireland, Iceland, Greenland and Labrador to a triumphant welcome at Chicago. By the time of their arrival on 12 July they had covered 6,065 miles in about 48 hours flying time. Keeping such a large number of aircraft together, especially through thick fog on the long flight from Ireland to Iceland, was a tremendous feat of navigation. One slight variation in the engine revolutions of an aircraft in tight formation could have caused a collision.

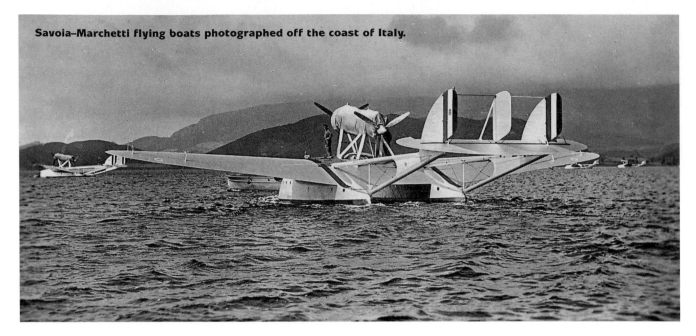

Savoia–Marchetti flying boats photographed off the coast of Italy.

The return journey via New York – where the airmen received a tumultuous reception – commenced on 19 July. The homeward route was via Newfoundland, the Azores, Lisbon (where another aircraft was lost and an airman drowned), and so back to Rome, where the 23 remaining aircraft arrived on 12 August 1933. Mussolini welcomed the airmen as they stepped ashore, and at an official reception the following day, after a triumphant procession through Rome, they were received by the King of Italy. The commander on both this flight and the South American trip, General Italo Balbo, had come to prominence both as a born leader and a fanatical supporter of Mussolini when a soldier during World War I. Mussolini appointed him Secretary of

State for Air in 1926, despite his complete lack of knowledge of aviation. After learning to fly and navigate, Balbo set about modernising the Italian Air Force, bringing it up to a very high standard.

It is a tribute to both Balbo's organisation and Italian engineering that such a flight could be planned and executed when an Atlantic flight of only one aircraft was considered a major event. For example, whereas other aviators had finished lost or well off-course on the long stretch towards the American mainland, all the Italian aircraft remained on course and in squadron order. It is also noteworthy that none of the 48 engines used on this flight gave any trouble at a time when aircraft engines were not particularly reliable.

Balbo addressing the crewmen who took part in the Atlantic crossing.

Some of the flying boats that took part in the formation flight to Chicago.

Partly as a result of this second formation flight, Balbo's popularity with the Italian public reached such great heights that Mussolini saw him as a threat to his leadership. This reached a climax when Balbo said Italy should side with Britain at the outbreak of the Second World War. In

1940 Balbo, leading from the front as usual, was killed when his aircraft was shot down by Italian anti-aircraft guns. The Italian government described it as an accident. The Royal Air Force sent a wreath to his funeral as a mark of respect.

The Lindberghs' Lockheed Sirius seaplane.

One flight which would have far-reaching consequences as far as passenger-carrying flights across the Atlantic were concerned was that of Charles and Anne Lindbergh between July and December 1933. The aircraft used was a Lockheed Sirius seaplane which had a range of 2,100 miles at a cruising speed of 115 m.p.h. In 1931, using the same aircraft, they had carried out a survey of the North Pacific investigating possible airline routes to the Orient. In 1933, having left New York on 9 July, they followed a route via Newfoundland, Greenland, Iceland, the Shetland Islands, Denmark, Sweden, Finland and as far as Moscow, reaching Southampton on 4 October. Having thus surveyed possible North Atlantic routes they made their way back to New York surveying South Atlantic routes via Ireland, Scotland,

France, Holland, Switzerland, Spain, Portugal, the Azores and down to North Africa. Crossing the South Atlantic between Bathurst and Natal, they finally made their way home to New York, arriving on 19 December. Both of these survey flights were made on behalf of Juan Trippe, the founder of Pan American Airways. In the early 1930s, Trippe was working hard to build up a network of air routes throughout South America. He also had his eye on possible development across the Pacific, and at the same time was exerting pressure on European governments to allow him to establish regular services across the Atlantic. His plans were mainly thwarted by Imperial Airways – who had sole landing rights in Newfoundland – and lack of suitable aircraft.

Pan Am's *China Clipper* made history by flying from California to Hawaii as part of the company's transpacific route.

The vast number of passenger flights across the Atlantic today is probably due more to the influence of Juan Trippe than anyone else. Trippe was a devious character, described by President Roosevelt as a 'fascinating Yale gangster'. The Secretary of the Interior, Harold L. Ikes, called him 'an unscrupulous person who cajoles and buys his way'. Even a Trippe supporter had to admit that he was the sort of person who 'if the front door was open . . . would go in by the side window'. Trippe was born into a family with connections to most of the millionaires and influential business people of his day. His mother had desperately wanted a daughter, who she planned to name Juanita, so her son was named Juan instead. Many a deal was struck in South America because he was thought to have Latin American ancestry.

From 1931, starting with *American Clipper* (a Sikorsky S40 flying boat) and throughout the airline's life, all Pan Am's aircraft were called Clippers. The crew had naval officer type uniforms, were given naval ranks, and were expected to maintain the highest possible standards of smartness. By the end of 1935, Trippe had inaugurated the first transpacific airline service, and by 1937 Pan American were operating services throughout Latin America. Juan Trippe also had control of the China National Aviation Corporation operating in China, Japan and India.

Trippe was also keen to inaugurate North Atlantic flights, but was held back by the British, who did not want the Americans to start a service before they were ready themselves. They were able to block Trippe's plans by withholding landing rights in Newfoundland. However, with the Lindberghs' survey flights completed, the lack of landing rights in Newfoundland was only a minor obstacle to someone with Trippe's determination. Eventually, after considerable pressure, arrangements were agreed for simultaneous test flights by both Pan Am and Imperial Airways. Pan American *Clipper III*, a Sikorsky S42, left Newfoundland bound for Ireland on 5 July 1937.

The *Clipper III*.

Simultaneously a Short Empire flying boat, *Caledonia*, left Foynes, Ireland for Newfoundland. Both aircraft made uneventful crossings, the *Caledonia* flying on to New York. On its return to Foynes, the two crews met up before the *Clipper III* left for home. The Imperial Airways Empire flying boats, some of the most beautiful airliners of their time, were already in service to South Africa and Australia but did not normally have sufficient range for a non-stop Atlantic flight. The *Caledonia* was stripped of all non-essential items to enable the maximum amount of fuel to be carried. It is said that a high-ranking Irishman offered almost unlimited funds to be flown across to America in *Caledonia*, even if it meant sitting on the floor. He was told there was no floor to sit on!

The *Caledonia*.

By the mid-1930s the British aircraft industry was under great pressure to produce an aircraft with a range and payload capable of commercial Atlantic flights. Particularly as far as the conveyance of mail was concerned, there was intense competition from the German catapult mail services. Major R. H. Mayo, the technical adviser to Imperial Airways, suggested a practical solution. A great proportion of an aircraft's gross weight is taken up by the fuel load necessary for taking off and climbing to its cruising altitude. Mayo reasoned that if an aircraft could be carried to its cruising altitude and launched from there, its range could be substantially increased. The larger aircraft, called *Maia* in this case, carried the fuel necessary for both it and its passenger (*Mercury*) to take off. At an appropriate cruising altitude, the smaller plane was released with sufficient fuel on board to carry the payload of mail further than would otherwise have been possible. This idea was not new. In 1916, a small flying boat, the Porte Baby, designed by Lieut. Cyril John Porte, successfully launched a Bristol fighter in flight. The *Mercury* and *Maia* combination was known as the Short Mayo Composite.

Maia and *Mercury*.

Mercury being launched in flight.

A telephone link and indicator light system maintained contact between the two pilots up to the point of separation, and the launch was completed in three stages. On 20 July 1938, *Mercury*, air-launched near Foynes, flew to Montreal and on to New York. Newspapers were carried and for the first time were on sale in New York the day after they had been published in London. With no air launch to help her on her way, *Mercury* had to return to Southampton in short hops via Botwood, the Azores and Lisbon. Both on the Atlantic flight and an earlier record-breaking flight to South Africa, the pilot was Donald Bennett. He achieved fame in World War II as Air Vice Marshall 'Pathfinder' Bennett.

During the war *Maia* was used as a training aircraft and also as a passenger shuttle between Poole and Foynes. She was sunk at rest in Poole Harbour on 11 May 1941 by a German bomber returning from a raid with one bomb left. After a covert mission searching for U-boats in Irish coastal waters, *Mercury* was handed over to the Royal Netherlands Air Force. On 21 August 1941 she was finally scrapped at Rochester where she had been built.

Edwin Lund · Howard Hughes · Grover Whalen · H.P. Connor · R. Stoddart · Lieut. Thurlo
flight eng'r · Pilot-Owner · World's Fair · navigator · radio eng'r · co-pilot

Floyd Bennett field N.Y. HOWARD HUGHES in his Lockheed Monoplane
around the world in 3 days-19 hrs-14 min. July 10 to 14th 1938- To Paris 3641 mi.
Moscow 1675. Omsk 1380. Yakutsk 2177. Fairbanks 2456. Minneapolis 2441. & N.Y. 1054

Howard Hughes' Lockheed aircraft and crew.

There were two significant Atlantic flights in 1938 which pointed the way as far as passenger-carrying services were concerned. Between 10 and 14 July 1938, multimillionaire Howard Hughes, whose later claim to fame would be the *Constellation* airliner and the *Spruce Goose*, flew round the world in under four days. His aircraft was a 14-seat Lockheed 14 airliner, a standard machine apart from extra fuel tanks and additional navigation equipment. Hughes and his crew took half the time to fly from New York to Paris than Lindbergh had only ten years earlier.

A Focke-Wulf Condor.

On 10 August 1938 a Focke-Wulf Condor left Berlin and flew non-stop to New York. Within three days it was back in Berlin. This could be said to be the first flight between Europe and America by a modern airliner. It marked the beginning of the end for long-distance flights by flying boats – even before they had carried passengers across the Atlantic. The aircraft which made this historic flight was the prototype Condor and was subsequently lost in an accident at Manila on its return from a demonstration flight to Japan. Two Condors were used by Hitler as his personal transports, and two more were supplied to DDL, the Danish airline. They were used on the Copenhagen–Amsterdam–UK service until early April 1940 when one of them was impounded and used for a time by BOAC. Lufthansa planned a Berlin–New York service by Condor, starting in 1940.

Pan Am *Yankee Clipper*.

The days of pioneering flights across the Atlantic essentially came to an end in 1939 when Pan American Airways started the first regular commercial flights across the ocean using Boeing 314 flying boats. The first of these flights, carrying mail only, was made by the *Yankee Clipper* from New York to Marseilles via the Azores and Lisbon on 20 May 1939. The same aircraft inaugurated the northern route from New York to Southampton on 24 June and carried the first passengers on this route on 8 July. The first scheduled passenger flight, from New York to Marseilles, was by *Dixie Clipper* on 28 June 1939. The Boeing 314 had a range of 3,500 miles at a cruising speed of 180 m.p.h. and weighed 80 tons. The Stars and Stripes first appeared on Pan Am Clippers on 28 August 1939, shortly before the outbreak of war in Europe.

Flight deck of a Boeing 314.

The spacious flight deck of a Boeing 314 was reckoned to be larger than the passenger compartment on the well-known contemporary Douglas DC-3 airliner. In theory, the Boeing 314 could carry 74 passengers. However, the actual number was reduced drastically on long journeys, with the capacity limited to 34 on overnight sleeper flights. On the 2,500 mile San Francisco–Honolulu trip only 30 passengers could normally be carried. The return flight from New York to Europe cost $675, said to be roughly equivalent to twice the modern Concorde fare.

From 1939 until the time the USA entered the Second World War, the four Pan Am Boeing 314 Clippers were the only civilian aircraft carrying passengers across the Atlantic. In late 1941 they were joined by two of the updated model, the 314A. Throughout the war, these six aircraft covered many thousands of miles across the Atlantic, mainly flying via the Azores or the long route via Brazil and Africa. They carried both passengers and freight. None of them were lost through enemy action, and the only casualty was *Yankee Clipper* which crash-landed and sank in the River Tagus, Lisbon, in February 1943. The last Boeing Clippers were scrapped in 1950.

This rare photograph, probably taken in 1940, shows three of the four civilian passenger-carrying aircraft flying the Atlantic at that time. NC 18604, *Atlantic Clipper*, is missing. The location is Faial, Azores.

In 1940 Pan Am were planning an experimental service for mail and express goods from the USA to Croydon. Had it gone ahead, this would have been the first transatlantic flight by a pressurised aircraft – the Boeing 307 Stratoliner. Being pressurised allowed the aircraft to fly 'above the weather' and take advantage of the stronger west to east winds at higher altitudes. The Stratoliner had a cruising altitude of 19,000 feet compared with the Focke-Wulf Condor, which cruised at 9,845 feet.

A Pan Am Boeing 307 Stratoliner.

Imperial Airways had hoped to operate reciprocal services across the Atlantic to match those of Pan Am, and had Short Empire flying boats *Cabot*, *Caribou*, *Connemara* and *Clyde* ready for Atlantic trials by May 1939. However, the intended date for introducing the service was delayed due to problems with carburettor icing. As a stopgap measure, *Cabot* and *Caribou* were stripped bare of all interior furnishings and modified for in-flight refuelling. On 5 August 1939 *Caribou* was refuelled in flight from a Handley Page Harrow tanker belonging to Sir Alan Cobham's Flight Refuelling Company, based at Shannon. Fifteen successful flights were completed before the service (used to transport mail) was discontinued. Passengers were never carried when in-flight refuelling was carried out. The process at the time involved rockets, grappling hooks, long cables and hosepipes. Fuel also flooded the bilges of the flying boats, representing a considerable risk of fire. In its modern guise, Cobham PLC is still involved in in-flight refuelling and a wide range of other aviation projects. In-flight refuelling played a major part in Britain's victory in the Falklands conflict.

***Caribou* being refuelled from a Handley Page Harrow during a test flight over the Solent.**

In 1941 BOAC purchased three Boeing 314A flying boats from Pan Am for $1 million each. These aircraft, G-AGBZ *Bristol*, G-AGCA *Berwick* and G-AGCB *Bangor*, made more than 200 Atlantic flights covering over a million miles during the war. They also flew briefly between Foynes, Ireland and Lagos, Nigeria on the BOAC route to Australasia. In January 1942, whilst bringing Winston Churchill home from Norfolk, Virginia via Bermuda, *Berwick* was intercepted by a formation of Hurricane fighters as a hostile, unidentified aircraft. The three 314As were sold to World Airways in 1948.

BOAC Boeing 314A *Bangor*.

The pioneer phase of transatlantic flights ended with the introduction of regular commercial services across the Atlantic and the start of World War II. The last three pioneer flights of this era all ended in disaster. On 17 May 1939 a Swedish pilot named Backman tried to reach Stockholm from Gander, Newfoundland, in a Monocoupe. He disappeared without trace. Thomas Smith left Old Orchard, Maine in an Aeronca called *Chief* on 28 May 1939 bound for Dublin. He was never seen again, but the wreckage of his monoplane was found in Newfoundland during the war. It had been powered by a 60 h.p. engine, the smallest used for such a flight up until then. The last attempt took place on 11 August 1939 from Cape Breton Island, Nova Scotia. Alan Loeb and Dick Decker were lost without trace, along with their Ryan Brougham – another light aircraft.

However, let us end the story of pioneer Atlantic flights on a brighter note, with the tale of Douglas Corrigan, a pilot who claimed he had no intention of flying the Atlantic and did so entirely 'by mistake'. By 1938, the authorities had cracked down on the large number of people with crackpot ideas about crossing the Atlantic, most of whom intended to fly in unsuitable aircraft with little planning. Too many of these flights ended in failure, loss of life and expensive rescue missions. As his ten-year-old, very second-hand Curtiss Robin was far too small for such a flight, Douglas Corrigan had no chance of a permit. However, he was given permission for a cross-country flight to Los Angeles. On 18 July, his tanks brimming with 218 gallons of fuel costing $66 including tax, Corrigan headed west from New York.

Corrigan's Curtiss Robin.

In his book, *That's My Story*, he recalls that after ten hours his feet felt cold. He discovered that he had a fuel leak and petrol was running down on his shoes. Worried that this would leak out onto the exhaust pipe, with disastrous results, he punched a hole in the floor away from the exhaust with a screwdriver. After flying for about 26 hours above the clouds, and concerned about ice forming on his wings, he came down 'lower all the time expecting to see a mountain come poking up through the clouds at any minute. Then at 3,500 feet I came down out of the clouds and saw nothing but water underneath'. It was then that Corrigan found he had been following the wrong end of his compass needle and had been flying east instead of west. So that is how, 21 hours after leaving New York, a small, battered aircraft came to land at Dublin.

Of course, nobody believed Corrigan and the whole nation laughed at his exploits. He was appointed president of the Liars Club of America. He had to be punished, and whilst returning home on the US liner *Manhattan*, he was handed a telegram which ended with the words 'your pilot's license is hereby suspended until 4 August'. The boat was due to dock in New York on 4 August! Corrigan kept his faithful Robin until he died recently, aged over 80.

"Douglas Corrigan and His $900 Crate"

Corrigan and his plane.

DOUGLAS F. CORRIGAN and his 1929 Curtis-Robins Plane NEW YORK to DUBLIN July 17-18, 1938 3150 miles 28 hrs. 13 min.

A blurred but rare photograph of Douglas Corrigan and his plane.

Airships

As far as Atlantic crossings are concerned, the airship story starts with the flight to America by the British airship R34 in 1919. R34 was a replica of the German Zeppelin L-33, forced to land in East Anglia in September 1916 after an attack by British fighters. Up until this time British attempts to make a large, rigid airship had been unsuccessful. With a diameter of 80 feet, the R34 was over 600 feet in length, longer than two football pitches. It made a double crossing of the Atlantic in 1919 to demonstrate the capabilities of airships in America, which had not seen a rigid airship in flight at that time.

With a maximum speed of only 65 m.p.h., the R34 took over four days to reach New York. (At times it could not achieve more than 35 m.p.h.) On arrival it was found that no one in America had experience of supervising the 600 men required for landing the airship, so Major J. E. M.

Pritchard was parachuted down, thus becoming the first visitor to the United States to arrive by air (and by parachute). According to Grover Loening, the American aircraft manufacturer, writing in his book *Take Off Into Greatness* (1968): 'As the ship floated stationary over the field at an altitude of 1,000 feet, a sudden burst of white fell from its control cabin. In a moment the object opened into a parachute and with a sangfroid and a chic that only the English can put over, the executive officer of the R34, Squadron Leader Pritchard, landed lightly and unconcerned in full beribboned uniform carrying a swagger stick.' Later Loening went on to say that: 'In photos and when first seen, [the R34] seemed a massively strong structure, justifying the name of "rigid". But close up one was astounded to see how the frame squeaked, bent and shivered with the cloth covering almost flapping in wind gusts.'

A composite postcard comparing R34's size to that of the Houses of Parliament.

R34 photographed after making its Atlantic crossing, with a picture of its commander, Major G. H. Scott.

To save weight on the Atlantic crossing, three men who had flown with the airship on previous flights were left behind (along with Major G. H. Scott's dog). A crew of 30 travelled on the airship, accompanied by Wopsie the cat, who was smuggled aboard as a mascot. Crew-members, along with various high-ranking VIPs, slept in hammocks slung both sides of a ten inch wide gangway positioned amidst the 5,000 gallon fuel tanks and bags of highly inflammable hydrogen gas. The fabric below the gangway would not support a person's weight if they fell onto it. In fact, in an emergency the crew were trained to escape by jumping through the fabric feet first.

In addition to the official crew, there was also a stowaway on board, Aircraftsman Bill Ballentyne, aged 22. After an initial threat to 'push him out with a parachute' as he was 'eating our grub', he was allowed to work his passage.

On arrival in America, most of R34's crew were unshaven and very dirty, and had great difficulty meeting the standards of smartness expected of British servicemen. In *Airship: The Story of the R34* it is recorded that: 'Lieutenant Luck, indulging himself in a rare wash, speculated grimly on the number of men using the same basinful of water – before him as well as after'. Major Pritchard did in fact shave before he was unceremoniously pushed through the window of the forward car for his descent to earth by parachute. Hot water was hastily obtained from an engine radiator for the purpose.

Sleeping hammocks and an access gangway on R34.

R34's control cabin. Ballast control levers and the ballast chart are both marked.

Airships were able to become airborne because the gas with which they were filled (initially hydrogen, and later helium) was lighter than air. Their shape meant that when they were propelled forward aerodynamic lift was generated. As with aircraft, this lift was controlled using rudders and elevators on the tail fins. A crude method of gaining height involved dropping vast quantities of water ballast – a normal amount to drop would be half a ton (about 110 gallons). In a typical rigid airship such as R34, the gas capacity was approximately five million cubic feet. The gas was contained in bags lined with a million gold-beater's skins (the technical term for the outer layer of the large intestine of an ox). Rigid airships consisted of gas bags contained inside a metal framework with an outer fabric cover stretched over the frame, whereas unrigid versions were essentially large balloons.

Bert Evendon, 'Sergeant Engineer, Aft Car' celebrated the sixtieth anniversary of R34's double Atlantic flight by crossing the Atlantic on Concorde in 1979. Following an illustrious career during which he had reached the rank of Wing Commander, Bert, then aged 86, was one of only three survivors from the original flight.

A photograph of R34 signed by Bert Evendon, an engineer on the transatlantic flight.

The Germans were pioneers of airship construction, and the name Zeppelin is synonymous with airships. The first name which comes to mind when Zeppelins are mentioned is that of the infamous LZ129 *Hindenberg*. However, there was another Zeppelin which deserved to be equally famous, LZ127, called the *Graf Zeppelin*. At the time of the *Hindenberg* disaster in 1937, the *Graf Zeppelin* had been carrying passengers across the Atlantic for over eight years. In *The Conquest of the Atlantic by Air*, published in 1930, Charles Dixon predicted that within ten years there would be a regular air service across the Atlantic. He prophesied that this would be operated using flying boats such as the Dornier Do X. On the subject of airships he said: 'I would hesitate to forecast their future in the first Atlantic services. One has not been built which could be considered as suitable for regular passenger and freight conveyance over such a distance with any chance of being profitable.' This forecast is interesting, as in the years immediately after Dixon wrote it Zeppelins seemed to prove him wrong, although the introduction of a regular transatlantic flying boat service in 1939 (by Pan American Airways) gives his theory credence.

The *Graf Zeppelin* and the Dornier Do X flying boat, the two largest craft of their types, c.1930.

A postcard commemorating the *Graf Zeppelin*'s historic round the world flight in 1929.

Historische Erste Weltreise des Luftschiffes „Graf Zeppelin" (L. Z. 127) in 20 Tagen
Landung in Friedrichshafen am 4. September 1929

Twenty passengers were carried in the height of luxury on the *Graf Zeppelin*, with sleeping accommodation in twin-berth cabins. A wide sofa converted into a second bed at night. The cabins were tastefully furnished with folding chairs, folding tables at the windows and ample cupboard space. At mealtimes the saloon tables were decorated with fresh flowers. It has been estimated that a single transatlantic fare would have cost the equivalent of about $5,000 at today's prices. However, it has also been said that the *Graf Zeppelin*'s economics were no more impractical than those of Concorde. In *The Zeppelin*, Christopher Chant writes of the *Graf*: 'A handsome saloon served as a lounge and dining room where, as in the cabins, the windows could be opened. . . . The catering staff, assisted by electricity, provided passengers with meals comparable to those served on a luxury liner.' The *Graf Zeppelin* was 100 feet in diameter and 776 feet long, longer than three Jumbo jets.

The *Graf Zeppelin*'s maiden voyage to the United States in October 1928 nearly ended in disaster. In a sudden rain squall the airship tilted violently upwards. The height coxswain desperately worked the elevators to bring the nose down, but the violent manoeuvre overstressed the control surfaces, stripping off the fabric. The airship had to

be stopped for emergency repairs, but fortunately these were carried out successfully. The incident happened at breakfast time and it was reported that a British passenger, Lady Grace Drummond Hay, had her breakfast emptied into her lap. A well-known journalist and socialite representing Hearst Newspapers, she was the second woman to fly the Atlantic after Amelia Earhart, and the first to do so in an airship.

On 1 August 1929, the *Graf Zeppelin* took off from Friedrichshafen bound for Lakehurst, New Jersey, to collect several passengers for the commencement of a round-the-world flight. It then returned to Germany, and with twenty passengers on board left Friedrichshafen on 15 August, flying non-stop to Tokyo (reached on 19 August). The *Graf Zeppelin* departed Tokyo on 23 August, flying across the Pacific to Los Angeles. At the start of its return journey from Los Angeles, disaster nearly struck the airship once more. After a successful launch, it sunk dramatically – to the extent that the bottom rudder fin struck the ground – due to a sudden variation in air temperature. However, following this incident the *Graf Zeppelin* made a safe return to Germany having covered a total distance of 21,200 miles in under thirteen days.

The 'Great Lounge' on the *Graf Zeppelin*.

construction commences.

tilting one of the rings.

the frame under construction.

the passenger cabin under construction.

the nose completed.

back ring assembly.

laying out the hull.

the tail end.

Construction of the "Graf Zeppelin"

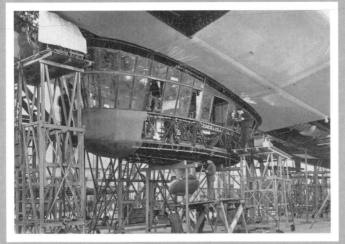

control gondola under construction.

painting the hull.

gas bags half full.

almost complete.

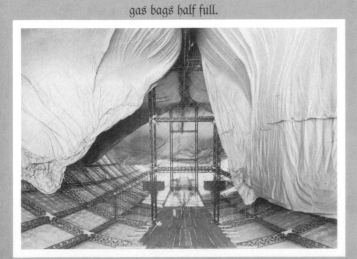

Graf Zeppelin approaching Rio de Janeiro.

Between 1930 and 1932 the *Graf Zeppelin* made eight proving flights to South America and back before commencing a regular service the following year. The northbound flight took about three and a half days; the southbound journey was slightly shorter. A wide variety of cargo was carried ranging from mail, the greatest source of revenue, to electrical instruments and machinery. On one flight a dismantled aircraft was carried, and on another an Opel motor car. Up to 200 lbs of precious stones were brought to Europe to be recut on return journeys. Another unusual cargo was queen bees. South American worker bees got lazy in the tropics and stopped collecting nectar to make honey, so queen bees had to be brought in from elsewhere for breeding purposes.

Up until the time of the *Hindenberg* disaster it seemed that airships represented the future for transatlantic passenger-carrying. Christopher Chant notes that between September 1928 and December 1935 the *Graf Zeppelin* made 505 flights and flew more than a million miles with very little trouble. On the day the *Hindenberg* tragedy took place the *Graf Zeppelin* was on its way back to Germany from South America. Wisely, the captain did not inform those on board of what had happened. When it was decided that as a safety measure airships should use helium gas instead of hydrogen, the *Graf Zeppelin* could not be converted. The pioneering airship was broken up at Frankfurt in March 1940.

This rare postcard (a composite image) portrays the *Graf Zeppelin* alongside the infamous *Hindenberg*.

Commander Ralph S. Booth

R100 and Squadron Leader Booth, captain on her Atlantic flights.

After the flight of R34 in 1919 it was eleven years before another British airship flew the Atlantic. The R100 and its sister ship, R101, were intended to rival the *Graf Zeppelin*. By the time they had been completed in 1930, the *Graf Zeppelin* seemed to have proved that airships – not aircraft – were the best way of carrying large numbers of passengers over long distances. Its only possible rival as far as aircraft were concerned was the Dornier Do X, still under construction and yet to prove itself on long flights. At this time airships had a far better record for Atlantic flights than aircraft. In the eleven years from 1919 to 1930, all seven attempted crossings of the ocean by airship had been successful. By comparison, 27 attempts by aircraft had resulted in sixteen failures and worse still, 21 deaths.

The story of R100 and R101 began in 1922 when Commander Dennistoun Burney, Conservative MP for Uxbridge, proposed that Britain should have a fleet of long range airships to 'join the outposts of the British Empire'. As a result, Vickers were given a franchise to build six airships for the routes to Canada and India. In 1924, when Labour came to power, a revised scheme was proposed involving the building of only two airships, R100 and R101. In order to ensure competition between the two airships and to encourage efficiency in both the public and private sectors, the R100 was to be built by private enterprise.

R100 was built at Howden, Yorkshire, by the Airship

R100 over Montreal.

Guarantee Company, a subsidiary of the Vickers Aeroplane Company. Due to various delays it was not completed until 1930, three years behind schedule. It cost £400,000. Neville Shute, later famous as an author, was employed as chief mathematician on the project. In his book *Slide Rule*, Shute describes Sir Dennistoun Burney, managing director of the project, as having 'a keen engineering imagination . . . coupled with great commercial sense'. One of the engineers who played a major part in the construction of the R100 was Barnes Wallis of Wellington bomber and bouncing bomb fame. The huge hangar where the R101 was built and the identical one used later by the R100 still exist, side by side, at Cardington in Bedfordshire. They are still used for the construction of small airships.

In *Slide Rule* Neville Shute gives a vivid description of flights on the R100 including that across the Atlantic and back. On a 48 hour test flight, he found the ship was flying over Lowestoft, off its planned route. On asking why he was told that the estranged wife of the third officer lived in Lowestoft. They had come 'as a graceful compliment' to empty their septic tank over the town.

Even when R100 was travelling at full speed, there was an area on top of the hull, just behind the curve of the bow, where the air remained still. It was a very pleasant place to sit and have a drink. A foot-wide gangway ran along the whole length of the hull on top of the outer cover (i.e. in the open air). Rope handholds were provided so one could walk from one end of the airship to the other. On one occasion (in flight, possibly 2,000 feet up and doing 60 m.p.h.) Neville Shute was very carefully crawling along this gangway when a 'rigger' came along, walking upright with his hands in his pockets. He stepped over Shute and carried on his way. Holes in the outer cover were always a problem on airships, and as a temporary in-flight measure large sheets of fabric with eyelets in the corners were used to cover them. Riggers, as the mechanics engaged on this

These dramatic construction shots show the frame of R100 suspended from the roof of the hangar.

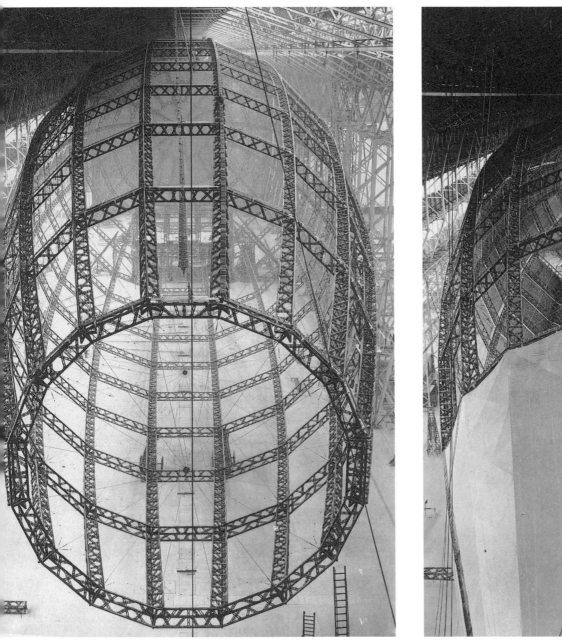

work were called, would climb about on the hull and stretch these sheets out over the holes, attaching them with ropes.

Neville Shute also recalls an incident when, en route to Montreal, the ship hit an air current. He describes how they were flying at a height of about 1,200 feet at a speed of 40 knots. The elevators were put hard down to stop the ship from rising, with the result that she ended up pointing nose down by twenty degrees. In that position she rose rapidly on the air current to a height of 4,500 feet, still with her nose pointing down. Supper was being laid out on the centre table in the saloon and it all shot off down the stairs, up the corridor, until some of it reached frame No. 2. 'I think the ship must have been at least 35 degrees nose down for a bit of cold meat or a slice of bread to get as far up the nose curvature as this', Shute wrote. They reached the specially built mast at Montreal on 1 August 1930, 78 hours after leaving Cardington.

Upon its return to Cardington R100 was, as Shute irreverently expressed it, 'put back in its box' next to the identical hangar where its sister ship, R101, was being prepared for its flight to India. The story of the R101 disaster makes fascinating reading. However, as this book is about flights across the Atlantic Ocean, I have reluctantly omitted it. Suffice to say at this point, only six of the 54 souls on board survived the crash of 5 October 1930, and in the wake of this all airship development work in Britain was abandoned. The R100 was broken up at Cardington in January 1931. It was flattened by a steam roller and having cost hundreds of thousands of pounds to build, its remains were sold for £450. This was a great pity as the flight to Canada had been judged a great success, and with a certain amount of redesign and modification the R100 seemed to have a promising future.

A reception was held in the airship's restaurant when construction was still at an early stage and before the gas bags had been fitted.

The *Hindenberg*.

At 804 feet long with a maximum diameter of 135 feet, the *Hindenberg* was the ultimate airship. It could initially carry 50 passengers (accommodated in twin-berth cabins), although in 1936 the capacity was increased and on the eighth flight to New York 75 were carried. The noise level in the public rooms was said to be far less than that inside contemporary cars and aircraft, and even luxury liners were considered to be noisier. The ride was very smooth and it was said that hardly anyone suffered from airsickness.

Accommodation was on two decks. 'A' deck contained a dining room, bar, smoking, writing and reading room, and included a specially-designed lightweight grand piano and 50-foot promenade deck with opening windows. Two staircases led down to 'B' deck and the passenger cabins (all of which had showers), plus twenty de luxe state rooms. The fixtures and fittings were even more luxurious than on the *Graf Zeppelin* while the presence of a smoking room was surprising considering the millions of cubic feet of inflammable hydrogen in the adjacent gas bags. The *Hindenberg* had been designed to use helium as the lifting gas, but following the refusal of the United States to supply this gas, she had to be redesigned to use hydrogen instead.

The modern lines of one of the *Hindenberg*'s public rooms.

Hindenberg refuelling at Lakehurst, New Jersey.

In 1936 the *Hindenberg* had a very successful year operating a regular service between Frankfurt and New York. It was on her first voyage to New York in 1937 that disaster struck. The cause of the initial fire is still in dispute, although the most popular theories are that a lightning strike or static electricity were to blame. Experiments carried out recently suggest that the fact that the gas bags were sealed with material containing zinc and magnesium may have been an important factor in the conflagration. A small burst of flame was observed, spreading rapidly to engulf the airship, which sunk to the ground in a ball of flames in less than a minute. It seems a miracle that 61 men and women survived the disaster, although 36 others were killed.

What horrified the world was that a radio commentator described the whole scene from beginning to end. This broadcast, probably more than anything else, led to the end of the use of airships for carrying passengers. Even if this disaster had not occurred, the days of the airship would have been numbered. In terms of manpower, airships were very expensive to operate. Almost as many crew members were required to man them as passengers were carried. The *Hindenberg* was said to require about half a square mile of open space to land and 250 men to control it on arrival; factors that probably meant an airport could only accommodate one airship at a time.

Das neue deutsche Zeppelin-Luftschiff „Hindenburg" L. Z. 129
Das größte Luftschiff der Welt.
Länge 248 m. Höhe 44,7 m, größter Durchmesser 41,2 m.
Vortriebsmaschinen: 4 Mercedes-Benz Dieselmotore von je 1100 PS Geschwindigkeit von etwa 130 Stdkm.

Catapult mail

It was obvious from the time of the first Atlantic flight that mail could be delivered faster by air than sea, and there were other occasions when sending documents by air could provide commercial gain. For example, there was considerable financial advantage in documents relating to a ship's cargo reaching port before the ship docked. In the 1920s, both in America and Europe, experiments were carried out to launch mail-carrying aircraft from ocean liners whilst at sea, and also to use aircraft to transfer mail to liners which had already set sail.

SS *Leviathan*.

On 1 August 1927 a biplane was launched from the SS *Leviathan*, then the largest liner in the world, using a specially constructed wooden ramp supported by stilts on the ship's bridge. The pilot was Clarence Chamberlin, and the flight took place only two months after his epic journey to Berlin with Charles Levine. His Fokker S-3 biplane required only 75 feet to take off, and the wooden 'runway' was 114 feet long. On the experimental flight, 600 letters were carried and the liner was 80 miles outbound from New York en route to Europe. (The purpose of this experiment was to demonstrate the feasibility of the system, rather than cut transit time.) The aircraft flew to Hasbrouck Heights, New Jersey.

Soon afterwards, on 20 August, an experimental flight was made to deliver mail to the *Leviathan* after she had sailed. However, the aircraft was unable to find the liner in dense fog. Other experiments were carried out involving both delivering mail to the liner and using an aircraft in flight to collect mail at sea, but further development was abandoned. (The procedure, known as the Adams Air Mail Pick Up system, was later used to collect post from isolated ground-based sites without the need for an aircraft to land.)

Chamberlin's Fokker aircraft prior to take-off from SS *Leviathan*.

The *Ile de France*.

In both France and Germany development was taking place on what was considered to be the logical next step for launching a mail-carrying aircraft from a liner: the use of a powerful catapult to supplement the engine power of the aircraft during its launch. This idea was not new, however, and power-operated catapults had previously been used on warships. Both the French and the Germans used compressed air to power their catapults.

The French were the first to operate a commercial airmail service across the Atlantic using aircraft catapulted from the liner *Ile de France*. Four flights were made in 1928, the first taking off from the ship and landing in New York. The second flight was launched from the *Ile de France* to Paris on the liner's return journey, and the third was from the ship to Boston. Unfortunately on the fourth occasion, having been launched on the return voyage to France, the aircraft was forced down off the Scilly Isles, although both the crew and the mail were recovered. Further flights were made from the *Ile de France* between 1928 and 1930, but the service was unable to compete with German catapult operations and the last flight from the *Ile de France* was made on 2 September 1930.

Following the success of flights from the *Ile de France*, agreement was reached between the German steamship company Norddeutscher Lloyd and Ernst Heinkel Flugzeuwerke AG to install catapults on the liners *Bremen* and *Europa*. These catapults were fitted on the sun decks of the liners between the two funnels. The catapult design, which dated back to 1922, formed the basis for that used on all German transatlantic catapult operations up to 1939.

The seaplane was positioned on a sled running on rails about 90 feet long. At the end of the rails, the sled stopped and the aircraft was launched. It was designed to achieve a flying speed of 70 m.p.h. after travelling only 65 feet.

A Junkers Ju46 positioned on its catapult on the *Europa*.

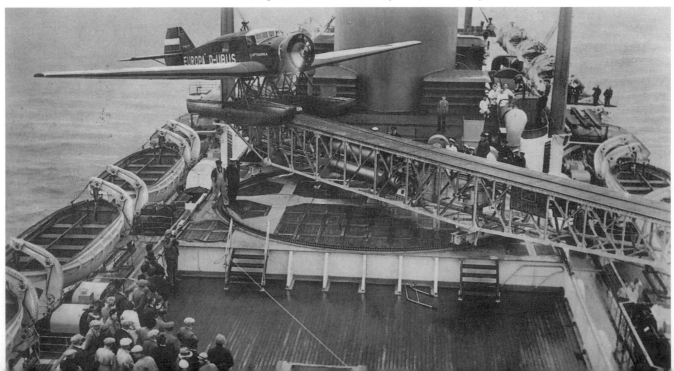

The *Bremen*.

The first mail-carrying flight to be launched from the *Bremen* was made on 22 July 1929 during the liner's maiden voyage to New York, on which she gained the Blue Riband for the fastest Atlantic crossing by a liner, beating by nine hours the record which had been held for 22 years by the British liner *Mauretania*. The original intention had been to launch the aircraft 500 miles out from New York, but the captain decided against this. If the plane had crashed on take-off, he would have had to carry out a rescue mission and thus jeopardise his record attempt. In the event, the launch was made only 50 miles from New York. The aircraft was a modified racing seaplane, the Heinkel He.12 two-seat monoplane. The crew were pilot Flight Captain Jobst von Studnitz and mechanic/radioman Karl Kirchoff.

On 15 September 1930 the same crew that had made the initial flight from the *Bremen* carried out the first official mail-carrying flight from the *Europa*. It had originally been intended that catapult flights from German liners should be launched about 800 miles from port, giving a time-saving of 24 hours. However, a later development of the catapult service involved the aircraft landing and refuelling en route after it had been catapulted, thus increasing the range and time-saving. On 8 September 1931, a record flight over a total distance of 1,500 miles was made from the *Europa*. After refuelling at Cape Breton Island, Canada and Bridgeport, Connecticut, the aircraft reached New York, giving the mail it carried an advantage of about 36 hours over transport by sea alone.

However, by 1935 the bulk of transatlantic airmail was being carried the entire distance by air via the depot ship and Zeppelin services, and so catapult flights from liners diminished substantially in number. Those from the *Bremen* and *Europa* continued on a reduced frequency until almost the outbreak of World War II in 1939. The last flight from the *Bremen* was on 23 August and that from the *Europa* on 12 August.

A Junkers Ju46 being launched from *Europa*.

The *Westfalen* (a converted merchant ship) with a Dornier Wal on the catapult.

As larger mail-carrying seaplanes became available, the idea of using depot ships was conceived. These depot ships, capable of taking a seaplane on board and launching it by catapult after it had been serviced and refuelled, were positioned in the mid-Atlantic.

The first sea trials of the system were carried out off Bathurst, Gambia on 2 June 1933. *Monsun*, a Dornier Wal (Whale), was launched from the depot ship *Westfalen*. After landing nearby, the aircraft was recovered by the ship and taken back to Bathurst. The recovery involved driving the aircraft on to a 'dragsail' (raft) towed by the ship from whence it was picked up by the ship's crane. On 4 June, *Monsun* flew from Bathurst to the *Westfalen*, which was repositioned at a new rendezvous 400 miles nearer South America. *Monsun* carried only the light fuel-load needed for the short flight to the ship. After retrieval the aircraft was refuelled with the necessary fuel-load for the longer transatlantic flight. On 6 June it was launched by catapult and flew to Natal, arriving the next day. For the return flight, the *Westfalen* repositioned off Fernando de Noronha.

Monsun on an
unidentified vessel.

The catapult developed 38,000 horsepower and the effect of all this power being suddenly applied to an aircraft normally requiring only 600 h.p. to take off can only be imagined. Suffice to say that it accelerated the aircraft to over 100 m.p.h. in only two seconds. The launch, followed by a long flight only 30 feet above the sea (to achieve an increase in cruising speed and a fuel saving), must have put the pilot under considerable stress. One pilot, Captain Cramer von Clausbruch, claimed that the ocean transfer involved a 'double refuelling' – a strong drink for the pilot as well as one for the aircraft.

Taifun, a 10-ton Wal, positioned on its catapult on the *Friesenland*.

In 1934, a regular service was introduced using two depot ships – the *Schwabenland* off Bathurst and the *Westfalen* off Fernando de Noronha. A more advanced aircraft, the 10-ton Wal, was employed on these flights. The use of depot ships at both ends of the transatlantic flight made greater payloads attainable. Later, two additional specially designed depot ships (as distinct from modified cargo ships), the *Ostmark* and the *Friesenland*, were introduced.

A Dornier 10-ton Wal, *Boreis*, being launched from either *Westfalen* or *Schwabenland*.

A Dornier Do 18.

Following a survey flight by a Wal from Hamburg to the Azores, four round trips were made between Lisbon and New York using the *Schwabenland* repositioned off the Azores. These were made between 5 September and 20 October 1936 using a Dornier Do 18.

Two Blohm & Voss Ha 139s replaced the Dornier Do 18 and made seven flights each way between 13 August and 20 November 1937 commencing from Lisbon. The catapulted stage of the flight was from Horta, Azores and the destination was New York. The four-engined Ha 139 was far more powerful than the Do 18 and could carry 1,000 lb of mail.

These flights made use of the *Schwabenland* and *Friesenland* positioned at each end of the long transatlantic stage.

This service was operated by Lufthansa at a time when their aircraft seemed to get lost very easily on the short flight from Berlin to Croydon (then the main airport for London). However, they always found their depot ship without trouble. It became apparent after the start of World War II that while they were 'lost' trying to find Croydon, German aircraft were photographing the surrounding countryside, probably including nearby RAF airfields and other military installations.

A Blohm & Voss HA 139.

South Atlantic flights

In view of their colonial interests in Latin America, the Portuguese were the first nation to take up the challenge of flying the South Atlantic. The first crossing, between Lisbon and Rio de Janeiro, was a long and difficult flight. It was a tribute to the bravery and determination of the crew, Portuguese naval officers Gago Coutinho and Sacadura Cabral, that it was completed at all. Their flight took them ten weeks and they survived two air crashes on the way! They took off in a British Fairey IIID seaplane from Lisbon on 30 March 1922. The first part of their flight, to Saint Vincent (Cape Verde Islands) via the Canary Islands, was completed without difficulty. However, higher than expected fuel consumption made it impossible to reach their next port of call, the islands of Fernando de Noronha. Instead they flew to a rendezvous point at two tiny uninhabited rocks isolated in the mid-Atlantic called Saint Peter and Saint Paul, where they had arranged to be refuelled by a battleship. Unfortunately, landing near the ship in rough seas, their aircraft was badly damaged and eventually sunk.

The crew were taken to Fernando de Noronha to await the arrival of a second aircraft by ship. When this came they decided to fly back to Saint Peter and Saint Paul where the first aircraft had sunk, so that they could claim to have flown the complete route to Rio. Unfortunately, on the way back to Fernando de Noronha, their engine stopped and they were forced to land on the sea. With the

A postcard commemorating Coutinho and Cabral's flight.

aircraft breaking up and no radio to summon help, they were in a predicament. To make matters worse sharks circled the stricken plane, even swimming beneath the floats. Around midnight, when all hope of rescue seemed gone, they saw the lights of a ship. The *Paris City*, bound for Rio, took their aircraft in tow and arranged a rendezvous with the Portuguese warship. The crew were taken on board the warship but it was not possible to save the aircraft.

Coutinho and Cabral's crossing of the South Atlantic was a source of great pride in Portugal.

A US published postcard celebrating the Portuguese duo.

In both Portugal and Brazil, public subscriptions were opened to pay for a third aircraft. However, as national pride was involved, the Portuguese government very reluctantly handed over its last remaining Fairey seaplane and sent it to Fernando de Noronha by ship. Eventually, after a flight down South America in four stages, Coutinho and Cabral reached Rio on 17 June 1922. Cabral did not have much time to enjoy his fame after the flight, being killed in a flying accident soon afterwards. Gago Coutinho later reached the rank of admiral and lived until 1960. It is a tribute to his skills as a navigator that – in spite of their difficulties – his estimated flying time, made prior to take-off, was within a quarter of an hour of their actual time of 60 hours. The aircraft in which they completed their flight is on display in the Portuguese Naval Museum in Lisbon.

The *Plus Ultra*.

Spain was soon looking for an opportunity for a long distance flight which would put Spanish aviation on the map, and the obvious choice was one to Argentina, an old partner in Spain's colonial empire. To gain further publicity, the flight started from Huelva, whence Columbus had departed for his Atlantic voyage. The aircraft was called *Plus Ultra* (Further Still); this was the phrase that had been used by King Charles V of Spain when America had been discovered. The commander of the four-man crew on the flight was Ramon Franco. His older brother Francisco later became famous as Generalisimo Franco, the dictator, following his victory in the Spanish Civil War. The navigator, Captain Ruiz de Alda, was a co-founder of the fascist Falange party. Lieutenant Juan Duran was the co-pilot, and completing the crew was mechanic Pablo Rada. A photographer started the flight with them, although he and Duran were offloaded at Cape Verde Islands to save weight on the next critical stage of their flight – to Recife – where Duran rejoined them.

The *Plus Ultra* was a Dornier Wal seaplane which had been built in Italy, as at the time of their flight (1926) Germany was prevented from building aircraft by the Treaty of Versailles. The Wal was a very practical aircraft for airline and other uses such as exploration, and a few remained with the Luftwaffe until as late as the end of World War II.

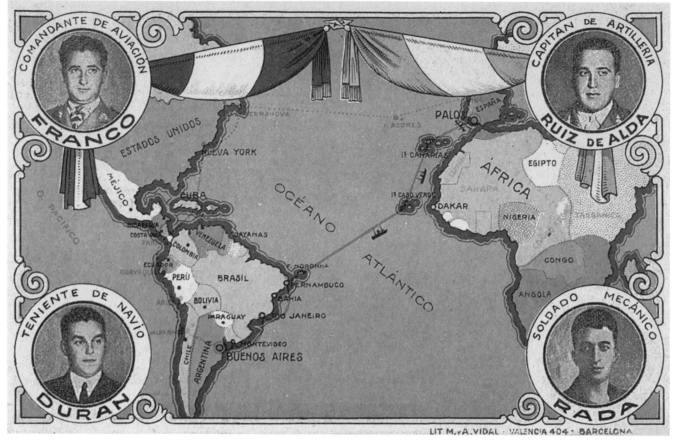

Route map of the Spanish flight.

The *Plus Ultra* left Spain on 22 January 1926 and arrived at Buenos Aires on 10 February. The total distance travelled was about 6,000 miles in a flying time of 51 hours. Franco and his crew had originally planned to fly non-stop from the Cape Verde Islands to Recife. However, to avoid a night landing there, they decided to land at Fernando de Noronha (these barren islands became known as 'the aviator's friend' due to the number of pioneer flights which landed there, often in trouble). In Franco's case it could have been a fatal mistake as the aircraft was damaged on landing in heavy seas. In great danger of being swept onto the rocky shore, he and his crew were very relieved to see some men launching a raft to come to their aid. They were wearing striped uniforms and were obviously convicts.

A Dornier Super Wal, the type of aircraft used by Franco on his second South Atlantic attempt.

With great difficulty, the rescuers finally got the aircraft safely moored to their raft. After repairs, Franco and his crew were on their way. However, after a while both engines started overheating. Struggling to stay in the air, they jettisoned as much fuel and water as they dared, frantically trying to reduce the weight of the aircraft. Eventually they reached Recife and flew safely on to Rio. They completed their flight to Buenos Aires without further problems.

In 1928 Franco made an attempt to fly round the world in a four-engined Super Wal, but damage to the hull caused an early end to his flight. On 21 June 1929 he made another attempt using a supposedly Spanish-built Wal but his aircraft came down in the sea. Amidst great national grief a frantic search was carried out by the navies of several nations. After several days he was picked up by a British aircraft carrier, HMS *Eagle*. Then his trouble really started. It turned out that he had switched the identifying numbers on the aircraft to disguise the fact that it was German and not Spanish-built. Franco was cashiered and imprisoned. He died in 1938 when his plane was shot down whilst on a bombing raid on the docks at Valencia. The fates of his other crew-members on the *Plus Ultra* flight were equally unpleasant. De Alda, the navigator, a prominent fascist, was executed by the Republicans. Co-pilot Duran was killed in a flying accident soon after their flight. Only Rada survived the civil war.

This imposing monument marks the spot at Buenos Aires where the famous Spanish flight of 1926 ended.

Between February and June 1927, an Italian Savoia–Marchetti flying boat piloted by the Marchese Francesco de Pinedo made a remarkable tour of both the South and North Atlantic Ocean. From Rome, de Pinedo and his crew flew across the South Atlantic to Buenos Aires via Dakar, Natal and Rio. They then flew north to New Orleans. Their intended route from there was up the west coast of the United States to San Francisco, Seattle and then east to New York. Unfortunately, near the Roosevelt Dam, a cigarette discarded by schoolboys in a rowing boat ignited spilled petrol on the surface of the lake where they were moored. The aircraft was destroyed and the crew had to wait a month for another one to be sent out by ship. They then flew back to Italy via Chicago, Newfoundland, the Azores and Lisbon, covering 28,000 miles in all in a flying time of just under 280 hours. De Pinedo was killed in 1933 on an Atlantic attempt when his vastly overloaded Bellanca aircraft failed to take off.

De Pinedo's flying boat, *Santa Maria*.

The squadron of Savoia–Marchetti flying boats over Rio.

The Savoia–Marchetti S-55X flying boat was one of the most outstanding aircraft of the early 1930s. Its twin-hulled shape and centre wing section made it ideal for dropping both bombs and torpedoes and also gave its machine guns an exceptionally wide range of fire. At the time Italy dreamed of dominating the Mediterranean, and it was decided that one way of demonstrating the might of her airforce would be to make a demonstration flight to South America. On 17 December 1930 a squadron of fourteen aircraft left Orbetello, Italy, bound for Rio de Janeiro. Following a variety of accidents, involving the death of five airmen, only ten aircraft reached Rio after a 6,540 mile flight. However, all returned to Italy and, having achieved its objective, the flight was fêted as a great success.

Between October 1927 and April 1928, Frenchmen Captain Dieudonné Costes and Lieutenant Commander Joseph le Brix made an even more sensational flight in a Breguet XIX biplane called *Nungesser et Coli*, after their friends who had been tragically lost on a North Atlantic flight (see pages 22 and 23). The flight commenced in Paris. After making what was thought to be the first direct flight from Dakar to Natal, they visited all the capital cities in South America before flying to New York via New Orleans and Washington. Following a flight to San Francisco they took their aircraft by sea to Tokyo. They completed their flight back to Paris via China and India in eight days.

It was subsequently concluded that the first direct flight across the South Atlantic had been completed in 1927 by Frenchman Captain Pierre de Serre de Saint Roman, accompanied by Lieutenant Mouneyres and an unnamed mechanic. This conclusion was reached in the light of wreckage found off the coast of Brazil which was thought to have come from their aircraft.

A souvenir of the Costes and le Brix flight.

Airmail was first carried across the South Atlantic by Frenchman Jean Mermoz, an employee of Lignes Aeriennes Latécoerè. The first delivery on the Buenos Aires–Toulouse route reached Toulouse on 13 March 1928, although the mail had been carried by sea between Natal and Dakar.

Mermoz's aim was to set up a weekly direct airmail service between Dakar and Natal. On his first flight (from St Louis, Senegal, to Natal) on 12 May 1930 he used a single-engined Latécoerè 28 seaplane. To allow time for mail to reach its destinations throughout South America and any

Jean Mermoz.

replies to get back to Natal, the return flight to Senegal was not scheduled until a month later. A length of the Rio Potengi river was selected for the take-off, as the seas around Natal were too rough.

Unfortunately the river was not wide enough to allow them to take advantage of the prevailing south-east wind which blew about 28 days out of 30. They made eight attempts to take off from the river on the first day, and after only three hours rest resumed their efforts. That day, 23 attempts failed.

Mermoz and his crew decided they would have to use another stretch of the river. A suitable location was identified about 30 miles upriver, and it was deemed that they should wait until the next full moon (7 July) before trying again. The cooler air at night was preferable to the tropical heat of the day, and the moonlight would aid visibility.

But the wind changed to westerly for the first time in a month and another series of failures followed. On 8 July Mermoz got a telegram instructing him to offload the mail, which would be sent by sea, but on his 53rd attempt he at last managed to take off. Unfortunately the crew's difficulties were not over. Engine trouble forced them to land on the sea near a weather ship 600 miles from Africa, and although the crew and mail were saved the damaged aircraft sank.

For his next flight to South America, Mermoz chose a three-engined Couzinet land plane, *Arc-en-ciel* (Rainbow). He did not agree with the French government's view that only seaplanes should be used for long-distance flights over water, arguing that in the event of a crash-landing at sea they usually broke up and sank just as quickly as land planes. This time Mermoz wanted the superior performance and efficiency of a land plane.

On 16 January 1933, the *Arc-en-ciel* made her first flight carrying mail from Paris to Rio via Dakar and Natal without any problems. On the return flight the port engine began leaking oil. However, the design of the aircraft made it possible for the mechanic to crawl through the wing and carry out repairs. Later, the same engine gave trouble and this time could not be repaired. Luckily the aircraft was able to fly with one engine out of action, unlike most multi-engined aircraft at that time. Eventually, losing height and speed, they reached the African coast safely.

The *Arc-en-Ciel* photographed in January 1933.

A postcard celebrating Franco–South American flights.

In 1934, the *Arc-en-ciel* was joined by a Latécoerè 300 flying boat, the *Croix du Sud*, and in that year the two planes made twelve commercial crossings of the South Atlantic between them. This was increased to a total of 36 in 1935. By then Mermoz had become a director of Air France, although he still flew the South Atlantic route. On 7 December 1936, a brief message was received from the *Croix du Sud* saying that a port engine had failed. The aircraft failed to reach its destination and no trace was ever found of it, Mermoz or its crew.

Formerly a Squadron Leader in the Australian Air Force, Bert Hinkler was one of those seemingly lunatic 'light' plane enthusiasts like Jim Mollison and Amy Johnson, who made long-distance flights in aircraft with engines half the size of anyone else's. By 1931 he had already broken long-distance records for flights between England and both Australia and Africa. For his South Atlantic flight he chose a de Havilland Puss Moth, similar to Mollison's. Hinkler left Toronto on 20 October 1931 with very little publicity and flew to New York. From there he made an over-the-sea flight to Kingston, Jamaica, where he arrived unannounced. (The main reason for not flying overland to Jamaica was that the US government would not grant him permission to fly over their territory as his aircraft did not comply with their safety regulations.)

After a week in Jamaica and other breaks en route, he reached Natal on 20 November. Setting out from there a week later, he battled against storms on the first solo flight across the South Atlantic, reaching Bathurst in 22 hours. He arrived in London on 7 December, and took off from England in the same Puss Moth on 7 January 1933. Hinkler intended to fly non-stop to Brindisi, Italy, as part of an attempt to beat the record for a light aircraft flight to Australia. When the snow melted in the Apennine mountains near Pratomagno, Italy, his body and the shell of his burnt out aircraft were found.

A rare photograph of Hinkler captioned 'Tour of the South Atlantic in Puss Moth, 1931'.

Index